Lernkrimi Englisch

Toxic Testament

Tracy Bowens

Compact Verlag

In der Reihe Compact Lernkrimi Classic sind erschienen:
- Englisch, Französisch, Italienisch, Spanisch: B1, B2
- Englisch GB/US, Business English: B1, B2
- Deutsch: B1
- Sammelband Lernkrimi Englisch, Französisch, Spanisch: B1/B2

In der Reihe Compact Lernkrimi Kurzkrimis sind erschienen:
- Englisch, Französisch, Italienisch, Spanisch: A2, B1, Deutsch: A2

In der Reihe Compact Lernkrimi History sind erschienen:
- Englisch: B1, B2, Italienisch: B1

In der Reihe Compact Lernthriller sind erschienen:
- Englisch: B1, B2, Spanisch: B1

In der Reihe Compact Lernstory Mystery sind erschienen:
- Englisch: B1, B2

In der Reihe Compact Lernkrimi Hörbuch sind erschienen:
- Englisch: B1, B2, Business English: B2
- Französisch, Italienisch, Spanisch: B1

In der Reihe Compact Lernkrimi Audio-Learning sind erschienen:
- Englisch: A2, B1, Französisch, Spanisch, Italienisch: B1

In der Reihe Compact Lernkrimi Sprachkurs sind erschienen:
- Englisch, Spanisch: A1/A2

Lernziele:
- Grundwortschatz, Grammatik (A2, B1)
- Aufbauwortschatz, Konversation (B2)

In der Reihe Compact Schüler-Lernkrimi sind erschienen:
- Englisch, Französisch, Spanisch, Latein, Deutsch, Mathematik, Physik, Chemie
- Sammelband Schüler-Lernkrimi Englisch

Weitere Titel sind in Vorbereitung.

Redaktion: Helga Aichele
Fachredaktion: Nathalie Russell
Produktion: Wolfram Friedrich
Titelillustration: Karl Knospe
Typographischer Entwurf: Maria Seidel
Umschlaggestaltung: Carsten Abelbeck

ISBN 978-3-8174-7879-8
7278792

Besuchen Sie uns im Internet: www.compactverlag.de, www.lernkrimi.de

Vorwort

Mit dem neuen, spannenden Compact Lernkrimi können Sie Ihre Englischkenntnisse auf schnelle und einfache Weise vertiefen, auffrischen und überprüfen.

Inspector Hudson erleichtert das Sprachtraining mit Action und Humor.

Der Krimi wird durch abwechslungsreiche und kurzweilige Übungen ergänzt, die das Lernen unterhaltsam und spannend machen. Prüfen Sie Ihr Englisch in Lückentexten, Zuordnungs- und Übersetzungsaufgaben, in Buchstabenspielen und Kreuzworträtseln!

Ob im Bus oder in der Bahn, im Wartezimmer, zu Hause oder in der Mittagspause – das Sprachtraining im handlichen Format bietet die ideale Trainingsmöglichkeit für zwischendurch.

Schreiben Sie die Lösungen einfach ins Buch!

Die richtigen Antworten sind in einem eigenen Lösungsteil am Ende des Buches zusammengefasst. Im Anhang befindet sich außerdem ein Glossar, in dem die schwierigsten Wörter übersetzt sind. Diese sind im Text kursiv markiert.

Und nun kann die Spannung beginnen…

Viel Spaß und Erfolg!

Inhalt

Story

James Hudson arbeitet als Inspector bei der legendären Polizeibehörde Scotland Yard. Er ist einer der fähigsten Männer und wird immer dann zurate gezogen, wenn seine Kollegen mal wieder vor einem Rätsel stehen. Oft wird er dabei von Elvira Elliot, der jungen, attraktiven Versicherungsagentin unterstützt.

Der Unternehmer Sir Anthony Baker stirbt durch Herzversagen. Das sieht zunächst nicht nach einem Fall für Inspector Hudson aus. Doch am Tatort finden sich Hinweise, dass noch jemand im Zimmer war, als Sir Anthony starb. War es also Mord? Und warum mischt sich Sir Reginald in die Ermittlungen ein?
Schon bald stößt Hudson auf Intrigen und gut gehütete Familiengeheimnisse. Sir Anthonys Familie wartet schon begierig auf die Eröffnung des Testaments. Es gibt viele Verdächtige, doch erst durch einen weiteren Toten kommt Hudson der Lösung des Falls einen entscheidenden Schritt näher. Bei der Verlesung des Testaments überschlagen sich schließlich die Ereignisse…

Chapter 1: Shared Pain

My arm is *numb*, Sir Anthony Baker thought as he rubbed his right arm. I can't feel a thing. All of the pain is in my *chest*.

Sir Anthony closed his eyes. Images of his life *flashed by* as in a film.

Oh no, Sir Anthony thought. So it is true: you do see your life *flashing by* you when you're dying. But I want to live. I'm not ready to let those people get their hands on my money.

Sir Anthony Baker had felt the same pain before. Over the years his heart had got weaker and weaker. His doctor had told him to *avoid* stress and to *improve* his *diet*. But Sir Anthony liked to *live life to the full*. He wasn't very good at following orders.

"I can see that you aren't feeling very well," Sir Anthony heard someone say.

He *blinked*. A person was standing on the other side of the desk.

You might be waiting for me to die, but you are not going to *get rid of* me that easily, he thought bitterly.

Grimacing with pain, Sir Anthony opened his desk *drawer*. His hand searched for his heart pills.

Where are they? I know I put a bottle in here.

His hand moved faster. The pain in his *chest* was growing stronger. Suddenly he heard the sound of pills rolling around in a bottle. For a moment, he felt *relief* instead of panic. Sir Anthony could hear the pills, but he still could not feel the bottle.

The person standing on the other side of the desk shook the bottle of pills again.

"If I were you, I would give up," the person laughed. "I'm enjoying watching you *suffer*. Now you know how I've felt all my life."

Sir Anthony saw another face. He knew it from somewhere…

"I want this to be the last face you see before you die."

Sir Anthony opened his mouth, but no words came out. He *blinked* once more before closing his eyes for the last time.

ÜBUNG 1

Übung 1: Wie heißt der Begriff auf Deutsch? Übersetzen Sie!

1. numb ______________________
2. improve ______________________
3. suffer ______________________
4. grimace ______________________
5. flash by ______________________
6. relief ______________________
7. diet ______________________
8. chest ______________________

Inspector James Hudson was enjoying a relaxing Saturday afternoon reading the London Times. He liked reading news that was not about the *cases* he was *investigating*. Seeing news about his *cases* was something Inspector Hudson was used to. He had noticed a long time ago that bad news often made the *headlines* while good news was reserved to a small article on page two.
Usually, Inspector Hudson did not need to read the newspaper to know if he had made the *headlines* or page two. *Headline* stories were often *accompanied* by an invitation to talk to his boss, Sir Reginald, in Sir Reginald's office. When stories *appeared* on the second page, he only received a phone call from Sir Reginald thanking him for all his hard work.

Leafing through the paper, Inspector Hudson decided that it was time to get out of the house. The day was bright and sunny. Why read about the happenings in London when one could *experience* them *first-hand*?

Übung 2: Schreiben Sie die Sätze um! Verwenden Sie dabei ein Adverb.

1. Inspector Hudson was happy reading the paper.

Inspector Hudson was reading the paper happily.

2. Hudson had a quick look at the front page.

3. Hudson listened to Sir Reginald with patience.

4. He was slow to rise.

5. The sunshine was bright.

6. Hudson was comfortable in his chair.

As he was about to rise from his chair, Hudson heard the phone ring. I hope that's for Miss Paddington and not me, he thought, even though he knew that it was *unlikely*. His housekeeper had trained her friends and family to phone her on her mobile phone. *According to* Miss Paddington, Inspector Hudson's *line* was to be kept for important calls *summoning* him to *crime scenes*.

The phone stopped ringing and Inspector Hudson heard Miss Paddington talking to someone. A few seconds later she was knocking on the library door.

"Just what I was afraid of," Inspector Hudson *mumbled*. "What is it, Miss Paddington?" he asked out loud.

"Sergeant Brooks is on the phone for you."

"Sergeant Brooks?" Hudson was surprised to hear that Sir Reginald was not on the other end of the *line*.

"Is there an echo in here?" Miss Paddington asked *irritably*. "That's what I said. He said that it's *urgent*."

Inspector Hudson put the paper down, walked to the telephone in the hallway and prepared himself for bad news.

"Brooks, what can I do for you?"

"Sorry to *bother you*, sir, but there's been a death at the Baker *residence* that we think you should take a look at."

"Does Sir Reginald know about this?"

"He knows, sir. The *victim* is a friend of his. Tony Barrington also recognized his name. But the *circumstances* of the *victim's* death are not very clear." Sergeant Brooks *hesitated*. "We just think you should have a look before people *jump to* the wrong *conclusion*."

"We?" Hudson asked.

"Yes, sir. Both Tony Barrington and I would like you to take a look at the scene before we finish for the day. The *victim's* family doctor is a friend of Tony Barrington. He came to the house when he was told about the death. But he thought something was strange. He called Tony and Tony called us. Sir Reginald will never let us forget it if his friend was killed and we let the killer *get away with it*."

Hudson *sighed*. "No walk in the park for me today."
"What was that, sir?" a *confused* Brooks asked.
"Nothing, Sergeant Brooks. Give me the address. I'll be right there."

Übung 3: Lesen Sie weiter und unterstreichen Sie ein Synonym für jedes der Wörter in Klammern!
(1. large house, 2. crying, 3. policeman, 4. not normal, 5. dead body, 6. asked)

ÜBUNG 3 !

Inspector Hudson drove to Sir Anthony's *mansion* as quickly as he could without breaking the speed limit. When he arrived, he parked his Bentley behind several official vehicles. He heard the sound of *sobbing* coming from a window at the side of the *mansion*.
The young *constable* guarding the front door seemed to be ignoring the *sobbing*. He stepped aside when Hudson showed his *ID*.
"I'm glad to see you," Sergeant Brooks said as he met Hudson in the hallway. "I hope we aren't wasting your time on this one, but we've noticed a few strange things. And with the *victim* being a friend of Sir Reginald… Tony Barrington can *fill you in*. He is with the *corpse* in the library. This way, sir."
"And who is the *victim*?" Hudson *inquired*.

"Sir Anthony Baker."
Hudson thanked him and walked quickly towards the library. Standing in the doorway, he started to laugh. Tony Barrington was looking at a bottle of pills on the desk. His glasses hung *crookedly* on his nose as he leaned over the bottle. Barrington moved to the left, then to the right, and to the left again. Finally he *squatted* and studied the bottle face to face.

"It won't bite, you know," Hudson joked.

The sound of Hudson's voice made Tony Barrington lose concentration. He *bumped against* the table as he looked up. The pill bottle *wobbled* dangerously for a moment.

"Whew, James," Barrington said, smiling at Inspector Hudson. "I'm glad they didn't fall off the table. I left them there as a present for you."

Hudson *raised* an eyebrow. He knew that Barrington was a *forensics* genius, but he wondered what was so special about a bottle of pills.

I hope I haven't driven here on a Saturday afternoon just because Sir Anthony decided to kill himself, he thought.

"I know this doesn't look like a *case* for us," Barrington continued. "Sir Anthony died from *heart failure*. There's no *doubt* about that. But when his family doctor was here, he wondered why Sir Anthony hadn't taken his heart pills? They were right here in front of him."

"That's a good question," Hudson said as he walked around the desk.

Sir Anthony's body was *slumped* in the chair. Hudson *examined* it. Then he *squatted* as if he were sitting in the chair. He stretched his arm out, *reaching* for the pills.

"Just out of my reach," he said.

Standing up, he *stared* at the *corpse*. "It must have been terrible to be so close to the pills and not be able to *reach* them. I can't believe that a man of Sir Anthony's social status didn't have a housekeeper. Why didn't he call for assistance?"

"*Apparently* the housekeeper and the butler weren't in the house at the time," Barrington replied. "Sir Anthony had gone to play golf earlier in the day. He always gave his *staff* time off when he played golf."

Übung 4: Lesen Sie weiter und unterstreichen Sie die passende Variante!

"Who found the (1.) buddy/body?"
"They did. The (2.) housekeeper/homekeeper and the butler."
Hudson looked *thoughtful*. "Sir Anthony has an (3.) active/passive day playing golf. He comes home and has a heart attack. Seems like an *open-and-shut case*. So what aren't you telling me, Tony?"
Barrington smiled and (4.) fingered/pointed to the four glasses on the *sideboard*. All four (5.) glasses/bottles were facing downward. Two of them were dry, the other two were a little wet. Inspector Hudson *strolled* (6.) over/under to the *sideboard* and looked more closely at the *damp* glasses.

"Did you find any *fingerprints* on these two glasses?" he asked Barrington.
Tony Barrington shook his head. "The outside of the glasses were *wiped* clean. So was the bottle of pills. That's why Sergeant Brooks and I decided to call you. If you ask me, someone was with Sir Anthony when he started to have *chest* pains. Either that person tried to help him, was too late, panicked and put the glasses away or…"
"Sir Anthony and the other person had *had a fight*. Sir Anthony started having *chest* pains and his 'visitor' *intentionally* kept his heart pills away from him. Before leaving, the person in question *wiped* the glasses and put them back on the *sideboard*, hoping to *erase* any *evidence*."
"You see. Aren't you glad we called you in on this fine Saturday afternoon?" Barrington grinned as he spoke.
Hudson's *gaze* moved from the *corpse* to the bottle of pills and then to the glasses. He *frowned*.

"I have to *admit* that it seems as if *there's more to this than meets the eye*. Where are the housekeeper and the butler now?"
"In the kitchen."
"Ah, the *sobbing*."
"I think that those sounds are coming from the housekeeper."
"*Estimated* time of death?"
"Around three o'clock."
"So the housekeeper and butler found him after returning home from their Saturday off."
"I know what you're thinking. Maybe they saw something."
"Did they?"
Hudson's tone was hopeful, but he already knew the answer.
"No. They got home around four o'clock."
"Thanks, Tony. It's time for me to *pay a visit* to the kitchen."

ÜBUNG 5 !

Übung 5: Ordnen Sie die Buchstaben in Klammern zu sinnvollen Wörtern!

1. When was the (mdeatties) ________________ time of death?

2. There was no (nedvciee) ________________ of a break-in.

3. Sir Anthony was found (dselmpu) ____________ in his chair.

4. His (fastf) ________________ had taken the afternoon off.

5. Inspector Hudson (dretas) ________________ at the body.

Sergeant Brooks was sitting at a large table in the kitchen when Inspector Hudson entered. A *plump* woman and a *skinny* man sat on the other side of the table. For the second time that day, Sergeant

Brooks looked happy to see Inspector Hudson. He stood up and walked over to Hudson.
"The housekeeper and the butler, I *presume*?" Hudson said.
"Yes. Her name is Bonnie. His is Finmore. They are married to each other," Sergeant Brooks *whispered*. "She won't stop crying. Been like that ever since I got here. Maybe you can get more out of them than I've been able to," Sergeant Brooks said. He looked tired.
Bonnie and Finmore were watching the two men *curiously*. As they *approached* the table, Bonnie dried her eyes with a *tissue*. Finmore put his arm around her shoulders.
"If you're going to try to make us say we know something about Sir Anthony's death," Finmore said angrily, "you can go home. We've told this one here all we know."
Sergeant Brooks *glanced* at Hudson, looking frustrated.
"Good afternoon Bonnie and Finmore. You're right. I'm Inspector James Hudson from Scotland Yard. As you found Sir Anthony's body, I would like to ask you a few questions," Hudson said with authority.
"It's okay, Finmore," Bonnie *sniffed*. "What would you like to know, Inspector?"
"What time did you return to the house?" Hudson asked Bonnie.
"We've already told the other one," Finmore *yelled*.
Hudson gave Finmore a dark look, but his voice was calm. "Then you won't mind telling me either, will you?"
Bonnie *patted* her husband's knee. The gesture *calmed him down*.
"We returned around four o'clock," Finmore said.
"We always get back around the same time. Sir Anthony has lunch at the club but dinner is always served here. We like to have a couple of hours to relax before getting back to work," Bonnie said.
"Was Sir Anthony difficult to work for?" Hudson *inquired*.

"We've been with the family for quite some time. If Sir Anthony were difficult, we would not have stayed," Finmore replied.
"The family? Do other *members* of the family live here as well?"
"No. Only Sir Anthony," Bonnie answered sadly. "Sir Anthony's wife died years ago. He has two children, Stella and Michael."
"If you can call them that," Finmore added.
Hudson *detected disgust* in his voice.
"Did Sir Anthony not *get along with his children*?" Hudson asked.
Finmore *shrugged*. "I *suppose* they got along as well as any family."

ÜBUNG 6 !

Übung 6: Korrigieren Sie die falschen Wörter und schreiben Sie die Sätze richtig auf!

1. Bonnie is a plum woman.

____

2. Bonnie and Finmore are divorced.

____

3. She snifed as she spoke to Inspector Hudson.

____

4. I think there is more than meets the ear here.

____

5. Tony Barrington is a forensics dummy.

____

6. Finmore shruged in response to the question.

____

"Anyway, it's family business. We don't *gossip*," Finmore continued *haughtily*.

"This isn't *gossip*. It's police business."

This time, Hudson did not try to hide his *irritation*.

Finmore looked *sheepish*. "I remember Sir Anthony said that Michael wanted to have a family meeting today."

"Do you know what Michael wanted to talk to Sir Anthony about?"

"Something to do with the family business. But Sir Anthony told him it would have to wait. Saturday was his golfing day and he wasn't going to miss it to discuss decisions that had already been made."

"What decisions were those?"

Finmore looked at Bonnie. She *squeezed* his hand.

"Before you answer, may I remind you again that this is police business," Hudson warned.

After a few moments of *silence*, Finmore spoke. "I think it had something to do with the sale of the company. The Bakers own a very *successful brewery*. But of course I do not know everything that goes on in the family."

How many times have I heard that from the butler? Hudson thought. He smiled at Finmore.

"Of course, I'll ask Michael for more details."

Übung 7: Welche Übersetzung ist richtig? Ordnen Sie zu!

ÜBUNG 7

1. ☐ gossip	a) Brauerei
2. ☐ company	b) Entscheidung
3. ☐ meeting	c) brüllen
4. ☐ decision	d) Klatsch
5. ☐ brewery	e) Firma
6. ☐ yell	f) Besprechung

"I'm sorry, Inspector, but why are you asking all of these questions?" Bonnie asked. "Sir Anthony died from *heart failure*. Finmore and I called the family doctor when we found him. Now all of you are here. I don't understand. He wasn't murdered, was he?"
"Sir Anthony did die from *heart failure*, that is correct. But please *bear with me* – I only have a few more questions. Did Sir Anthony always play golf on Saturdays?"
Both Finmore and Bonnie nodded. Hudson waited for one of them to speak. When they didn't, he asked another question.
"Where did he go to play?"
"The Epsom Downs Golf Club," Finmore said.
"And who did he play with?"
"We can't tell you that, Inspector," Bonnie said.
"He didn't have regular partners?"
"Sometimes he did *mention* that he was going to play with someone specific. But other times he just went to the club and played with whoever was there."

ÜBUNG 8 !

Übung 8: Lesen Sie weiter und setzen Sie das richtige Wort ein!
(chair, mansion, mind, mention, arthritis, subject, questioning)

"And today?" Inspector Hudson continued with his line of (1.) ________________.

"He didn't (2.) ________________ any names, did he?"

Bonnie asked Finmore.

"No, he didn't say anything to me."

Bonnie suddenly changed the (3.) ________________.

"Would you like a glass of water, Inspector?"

"No, thank you, Bonnie."

"You don't (4.) ______________________ if I get some for Finmore and myself, do you?"

"Of course not."

Bonnie rose slowly from her (5.) __________________. Hudson wondered if she *suffered* from (6.) ______________________.

He also wondered how she managed to keep Sir Anthony's (7.) ______________________ clean all on her own.

"Does anyone else work here, other than you and Finmore?" he asked Bonnie when she returned to the table.
Bonnie *sipped* at her water. "No, there's just the two of us."
"Isn't housekeeping for a big house like this rather a lot of work for you?" Hudson asked Bonnie.
"It's a lot of work for both of us. But we manage," Finmore said.
"It is true that in the last few years we have sometimes talked about *retiring*. The work we do was fine when we were younger. But at our age it just means a lot of *aches and pains*," Bonnie said as she rubbed her back. "I have arthritis, you know."
"Now that Sir Anthony is dead, we can fulfil our dreams," Finmore said.
"Finmore is talking about our *retirement* dreams."
"And what are your *retirement* dreams?" Hudson *inquired*.
"We want to move somewhere warm. This weather isn't good for my arthritis, you know," Bonnie answered.

ÜBUNG 9 !

Übung 9: Lesen Sie weiter und setzen Sie die richtige Form des Verbs ein!

"Did you (1. tell) ____________ Sir Anthony about your dream?"

"Yes, he (2. know) ____________ about our plans," Finmore replied.

"And how did he feel about (3. lose) ________________ two such *irreplaceable* people?"

"He (4. want) ____________ us to stay on, of course," Bonnie said.

"We (5. not have) ____________ any definite plans, though. We just talked about it from time to time," Finmore added.

Hudson heard the front door close. "Who (6. have) ____________ keys to the *mansion*?"

Finmore *glared* at Hudson and hit the table with his hand. The sound made Bonnie *jump*.
"I don't see what this has to do with Sir Anthony's heart attack," Finmore *snapped*.
Hudson had not interviewed such a rude person in a long time. He saw Sergeant Brooks shift nervously from one foot to the other. *Tension* filled the air. Hudson took a deep breath and counted to ten before speaking again.
"I think that my question is a simple one to answer. I'll ask it again. Who has keys to the *mansion*?"
"All of us and the family," Finmore *hissed*.
"Who is all of us?" Hudson asked.

"Bonnie and me."
"Thank you, Finmore." Inspector Hudson rose.
He *motioned* for Sergeant Brooks to follow him. Hudson took one last look at Finmore and Bonnie as he left the kitchen. Finmore was *comforting* a *sobbing* Bonnie.
"Who's informing the family?" Hudson *whispered* to Sergeant Brooks.
"Sir Reginald said he would take care of it. He didn't want to alarm the family… yet. In fact, he said that he wanted us to keep this quiet."
"I see," Hudson replied.
Tony Barrington greeted the two men as they walked out of the kitchen.
"So? What do you think? Have we wasted your Saturday afternoon?" Barrington asked Inspector Hudson.
Hudson *patted* both Sergeant Brooks and Tony Barrington on the back. "I *suspect* that you gentlemen were right to call me. Now I have two mysteries to *solve*."
Sergeant Brooks *cocked his head* to one side.
"Two mysteries?" he asked.
Hudson smiled. "Yes, two. Who caused Sir Anthony's heart attack and why doesn't Sir Reginald want us to *investigate* it?"

Übung 10: Welche der folgenden Aussagen sind wahr? Markieren Sie mit richtig ✔ oder falsch – !

ÜBUNG 10 !

1. Sir Anthony got along with his children. ☐
2. Another person may have been with Sir Anthony when he died. ☐
3. Bonnie and Finmore wanted to work for many more years. ☐

4. Inspector Hudson was happy to receive Sergeant Brooks's call. ☐
5. Finmore was not happy to talk to the police. ☐
6. Sir Anthony was in good health. ☐
7. Inspector Hudson does not plan to investigate the case. ☐

Chapter 2: Fighting Words

Epsom Golf Club's main lounge was full of club *members chatting* over drinks. None of them noticed Inspector Hudson as he leaned against the bar, watching them. The receptionist at the front desk had said that he might be able to find the club's manager, Eric Winslow, there. Hudson quickly identified him as the *cheerful* man who was moving from group to group, *patting* club *members* on their backs and laughing at their jokes.
The two men had met once before when Hudson had come to see Sir Reginald at the club to discuss a *case*. He was about to *approach* the manager when two men entered the lounge and went to stand next to Hudson at the bar. The subject of their conversation made him stop.

ÜBUNG 11 !

Übung 11: Lesen Sie weiter und korrigieren Sie die Wörter in Klammern!

"Did they really (1. flight) ______________ on the golf course?" the

man standing (2. closet) __________________ to Hudson asked.

"They certainly did. Right on the 17th (3. whole) ____________.

Arthur, believe me, I wouldn't have believed it if I hadn't seen it (4. himself) ________________."

"I've (5. herd) ________________ that Michael isn't happy about the (6. stayed) ________________ of the family company," the man named Arthur replied.

"I don't know what it was about, but both he and Sir Anthony were really angry. I saw Sir Anthony pointing his (7. gulf) ________________ club at Michael. Luckily his caddy was able to hold him back."

"John, (8. shurely) ________________ you're *exaggerating*."

"I tell you, I'm not," the one named John said hotly.
"And Michael?"
"Sir Anthony's partners were able to *calm him down*. I think one of them was Sir Reginald."
"Ah, always good to have someone from Scotland Yard around."
Inspector Hudson could not believe what he was hearing. Sir Reginald had been *witness* to a fight between Sir Anthony and his son, Michael, just hours before Sir Anthony's death. Was that why Sir Reginald did not want an *investigation* into Sir Anthony's death? Did he think that the fight *upset* Sir Anthony so much it was what made him have a heart attack later that day?
Suddenly, the club's manager was standing in front of Inspector Hudson.
"What's this I hear about Scotland Yard, gentlemen? I see you brought a *representative* for protection," he said to the two men as he looked at Inspector Hudson.

"What? Is Sir Reginald still here?" the man named John asked as he looked around.

"Oh, no. He left a long time ago. I'm talking about this fine *fellow* here."

Eric Winslow *patted* Hudson on the shoulder and pulled him closer to the two men.

"Inspector Hudson, *if my memory serves me right*," he said *cheerfully*.

"That's right. Good to see you again," Hudson said as he shook Eric Winslow's hand.

"Hudson. I've heard that name before," Arthur said.

"Of course you have," John replied. "He's one of Sir Reginald's best men."

"What brings you here today, Inspector?" Eric Winslow *inquired*. "Sir Reginald was here earlier today, but he left around four o'clock."

"So I hear. Actually, I'm not here to see Sir Reginald. I would like to talk to you about Sir Anthony."

The two club *members* looked at each other. "We'll leave you alone," John said.

"If you don't mind, I would like to talk to the two of you as well."

The club manager laughed at the look on their faces. "I hope you haven't done anything that will ruin the *reputation* of the club."

"You should talk to Michael Baker if you want to save the club's *reputation*," John *mumbled*.

"Yes, he was always a wild one," the club manager said, suddenly less *cheerful*.

"Is there somewhere we can talk that's a bit more private?" Hudson asked.

"Yes, of course, Inspector. Why don't we all go to my office," Eric Winslow *suggested*.

Übung 12: Beantworten Sie die Fragen zum Text in vollständigen Sätzen!

1. Who did Sir Anthony fight with at the golf club?

---

2. Where was Inspector Hudson when he heard the conversation between Arthur and John?

---

3. When did Sir Reginald leave the golf club?

---

4. Why didn't Inspector Hudson greet the club's manager when he walked in?

---

5. When had Inspector Hudson met the club's manager before?

---

6. Where did the four men go to talk?

A few minutes later the four men were sitting in a large office. Arthur and John were *sipping* gin and tonics. Eric and Inspector Hudson were *sipping* tea.
"I'm sure you are wondering what all of this is about," Hudson said.
The three men nodded.

Inspector Hudson suddenly felt a little *awkward*. An official *investigation* had not been started yet. He did not want Sir Reginald to hear that he had been asking too many questions. But he also did not want the *trail* of a possible murderer to grow cold. Finally he decided not to hide the facts.

"Gentlemen, I'm sorry to tell you this, but Sir Anthony is dead."

John almost *choked on* his gin and tonic. Arthur put his glass on the desk in the front of him. Eric Winslow sat back in his chair.

"Sir Anthony… dead?" he asked.

"That fight between Sir Anthony and Michael must have been really bad," Arthur said to John.

"As I said, I didn't hear what they were saying," John replied. He seemed almost sorry for what he had said.

"Did you see Sir Anthony and his son as they left the club?" Hudson asked Eric.

"Yes. I didn't really speak to Michael. I saw him crossing the *greens*. He got in his car and *sped off*. Sir Anthony left much later. Sir Reginald must have told you that he, Stewart Watson and Tim Meadows had something to eat before leaving."

Hudson nodded. He did not want to *reveal* that Sir Reginald had not given him any of this information.

! ÜBUNG 13

Übung 13: Wählen Sie die passende Redewendung!
(if my memory serves me right, bear with me, flash by, cocked his head, there's more to this than meets the eye, jump to the wrong conclusion)

1. Please be patient and wait until I have questioned everyone.

Please ______________________________

2. Sergeant Brooks put his head to one side.

He ______________________________

3. If I remember correctly, you are Inspector Hudson.

If ______________________________

4. I don't want people to guess the wrong facts.

I ______________________________

5. There is more to this case than we thought at the beginning.

There's ______________________________

6. Images of his life moved quickly through his mind.

His life ______________________________

"Could you describe what you saw in more detail?" Hudson asked John.
"I didn't see anything until they started shouting."
"They?" Hudson asked.
"Sir Anthony and Michael. It was very unusual. That's why we, my partners and I, watched. We were one hole away. We were very surprised."
"The club doesn't *approve of* such *behaviour*, Inspector," Eric added.
"That's understandable," Hudson said. "So Michael and Sir Anthony were shouting at each other."
"Yes, but we couldn't hear exactly what they were saying. And then Sir Anthony *raised* his golf club. It almost looked as if he was going to *strike* Michael with it. But he just pointed it at him. Michael *grabbed* it. He seemed ready to have a *fist fight* with his own father.

Thankfully, Sir Anthony's caddy pulled Sir Anthony away. Sir Reginald, Stewart and Tim took care of Michael."

"And Michael left after that?"

"Yes."

Hudson turned to Eric Winslow. "May I speak to Sir Anthony's caddy?"

"Of course. It was probably Paul. Would you like to use my office?"

"If you don't mind. Thank you," he said to John and Arthur and gave each of them his card. "If you think of anything else, please contact me."

The two men rose and shook Hudson's hand.

"I'll get Paul," Eric Winslow said.

ÜBUNG 14 !

Übung 14: Lesen Sie weiter und ordnen Sie die Buchstaben in Klammern zu sinnvollen Wörtern!

"You mean I (1. htigm) ________________ have been one of the last people to see Sir Anthony (2. veail) ________________?" Sir Anthony's caddy, Paul, asked (3. pcsnioert) ________________ Hudson a few minutes later.

"That's very (4. kielly) ________________."

"*Good heavens*!" Paul *exclaimed*, unable to believe his ears.

"How was Sir Anthony when you last saw him?"

"Fine. I even saw him leave the (5. ubcl) ________________. He seemed to be as fit as ever."

"Was it hard for him to find (6. eeoosmn) ________________ to play with when he arrived?"

"Hard? No, it wasn't hard at all. The usual *suspects* were (7. twainig) ________________ for him when he arrived."

"The usual *suspects*?"
"Well, uh… yes, I *suppose* that wasn't a good *choice* of words," Paul *mumbled*, looking *embarrassed*. "Inspector, I would like to help you, but you know how it is in these places."
"No, how is it?" Hudson asked *innocently*.
Paul leaned forward until his head almost touched Hudson's.
"This is a very respectable place with an excellent *reputation*," he *whispered*. "The things people do and say here stay here, if you know what I mean."
"You don't have to worry, Paul," Hudson *whispered* back. "I've already spoken to your boss."
Paul seemed to relax. "Sir Anthony played golf here every Saturday. He usually played with Sir Reginald, Stewart Watson and Tim Meadows."
"The same time every Saturday?"
"Just about."
"Did anything special happen today?"
"You're talking about the fight with his son?"
"Yes. What did they fight about?" Hudson asked.
"About the company. Sir Anthony's son said that Sir Anthony didn't have the right to make such decisions with the family's *fortune*. Sir Anthony told his son that he didn't have the right to talk to him like that. He said that if he wanted his son's opinion, he would ask for it. And then he told him to never, ever *embarrass him*

in public again. Sir Anthony's son said that he hadn't even started to *embarrass him*. And then I almost thought they were going to start a *fist fight*."

"What happened then?"

"Well, we separated them and Sir Anthony's son left," the caddy said.

"How was Sir Anthony after that?"

"As I said before, he was fine. I think he had the best game ever after that. It's as if it gave him renewed energy…"

"No signs of heart problems?"

"None at all."

Suddenly Inspector Hudson's mobile phone rang.

"Excuse me," he said as he turned to answer it.

"James, what are you doing asking questions at Epsom Golf Club?" Sir Reginald shouted from the other end of the *line*. "No, don't start trying to explain now. I want you here at my London club immediately."

The *line* went dead. Hudson moved the phone away from his ear and *sighed*.

"That's all for now," he said to Paul.

ÜBUNG 15 !

Übung 15: Setzen Sie die Sätze in die verneinte indirekte Rede!

1. You don't have the right to make decisions about the family fortune.

He said I didn't have the right to make decisions about the family fortune.

2. If I want your opinion, I will ask for it.

He said ______________________________.

3. What are you doing at the Epsom Golf Club?

He asked ____

4. I haven't even started to embarrass you.

He said ____

5. I want you here at my London club.

He said ____

6. You don't have the right to talk to me like that.

He said ____

7. I saw him leave the club.

He said ____

It was dark when Inspector Hudson arrived at Sir Reginald's London club. After identifying himself, he was directed to Sir Reginald and two other men.

"James – you got here quickly. Have a seat," Sir Reginald said.

"I got here as quickly as I could, sir," Hudson replied as he sat down.

"Stewart, Tim, this is Inspector James Hudson."

Sir Reginald did not have to say another word. Hudson recognized the names of Sir Anthony's golf partners. He shook hands with the two men.

"We should be going," Tim said.

"Yes, my wife expected me hours ago," Stewart added.

After saying goodbye to Sir Reginald, the two men left.

Sir Reginald focused all of his attention on Hudson. "I received a call from the manager of the Epsom Golf Club today. He thanked me for *handling* the *investigation* so *discreetly*. Of course I didn't tell him that I didn't know there was an *investigation* into the cause of Sir Anthony's death. I *assume* you have a good reason for thinking that one is necessary."

"We found *evidence* at the death scene that someone was with Sir Anthony when he died."

The expression on Sir Reginald's face changed. "I see. What *evidence*?"

"Two glasses that were still wet. Also it is *suspicious* that Sir Anthony's heart pills were close enough for him to see, but not close enough for him to *reach*. The pill bottle didn't have any *fingerprints* on it. None. Not even Sir Anthony's."

"You're saying that someone simply stood there and let Sir Anthony die?"

! ÜBUNG 16

Übung 16: Ordnen Sie die Synonyme richtig zu!

1. ☐ discreet	a) agree with
2. ☐ renew	b) show
3. ☐ grab	c) argument
4. ☐ approve of	d) tactful
5. ☐ reveal	e) begin again
6. ☐ fight	f) take

"Or even worse: they knew about Sir Anthony's heart problems and angered him *on purpose*, hoping that he would die."

"I'm sure you've already heard about the fight Michael had with his father at the Golf Club. Have you spoken to him yet?"

"Not yet, sir, but I had planned to *pay him a visit* before receiving your call. You knew Sir Anthony. Why was his son so angry that he almost attacked him in such a public place?"

"The Baker family is not a happy one. But it wasn't always like that," Sir Reginald said sadly.
"I heard that you are close to the family," Hudson replied.
"I almost married Anthony's wife," Sir Reginald laughed. "I say almost, but I don't think I really had a chance once she met Anthony. He and I went to school together."
"And you remained good friends even after the two of them got married?"
"I was more than just their best friend. Their first son, John, called me Uncle Reggie."
Hudson smiled at the thought of a young Sir Reginald playing with a little boy.
"And where's John now?" he asked. "I've only heard people talk about Michael. Oh, yes, and Sir Anthony's daughter, Stella."
"John's dead. Died years ago, as did his mother. The family was never the same afterward."
Sir Reginald put his *forehead* in his hand and shook his head.
"What do you mean?"

Übung 17: Setzen Sie die richtige Präposition ein!
(at (2x), back, for, in (2x), of, out)

ÜBUNG 17 !

Sir Reginald looked (1.) __________ Hudson. "John was the good son (2.) __________ every way. The best grades at school and a sharp business sense. Michael and Stella are different. Stella's looks save her, but poor Michael… He has never been able to *live up to* Anthony's *expectations*. Look at his *behaviour* today (3.) __________ golf club – it was *shameful*."

"Do you think Michael could have gone (4.) __________ to Sir Anthony's house afterwards and continued the argument?"

"No. The two (5.) __________ them had finished (6.) __________ today. Michael had fire (7.) __________ him when he *marched* across the *greens*, but Anthony put it (8.) __________."

"Hmmm… it must be hard to *live up to* the memory of someone who has died. The dead can do no wrong," Hudson *mused*.
"The family has seen a lot of *sorrow*. In fact, some speak of a *curse*."
"A *curse*?"
"It's nonsense of course. The family has just had a lot of bad luck. First John's death. And then Agatha's, Anthony's wife. And now Anthony himself."
"Sir Reginald, I don't think a *curse* killed Sir Anthony. I think a person did. Let me find out what happened to your friend."
Sir Reginald nodded slowly. "*Bring* his killer *to justice*."
Inspector Hudson rose.
"And James –"
"Yes, Sir Reginald?"
"Remember to be *discreet*."

! ÜBUNG 18

Übung 18: Welches Wort ist das „schwarze Schaf"? Unterstreichen Sie das nicht in die Reihe passende Wort!

1. embarrassing, shameful, sheepish, respectable
2. fight, attack, hug, argue
3. know, guess, assume, think

4. partner, friend, enemy, colleague
5. poor, fortunate, rich, wealthy
6. grab, pick up, give, take
7. suspect, witness, murderer, victim

Hudson returned home to sounds in the kitchen.

Ah, Miss Paddington's heating up my dinner, he thought.

He sat down in his favourite chair in the sitting room. *Smoothing* his right eyebrow, he thought about the events *surrounding* Sir Anthony's death. He had been able to *convince* Sir Reginald that *foul play* may have been the cause of his death, but what *evidence* did he really have? The *damp* glasses? They only showed that someone had been in the house with Sir Anthony earlier in the day. The bottle of pills? Maybe Sir Anthony had been in too much pain to *reach* them. An angry son? What family did not have disagreements?

"I wish I had been able to talk to Michael tonight," Hudson said out loud.

"What was that?" Miss Paddington said as she entered the room. She was *wiping* her hands on her *apron*.

"Hello, Miss Paddington. I was just thinking out loud."

"You can do a bit more thinking over dinner. It's ready."

"I'm not really hungry."

"It doesn't matter. Your dinner is ready and so you must eat it. You can't let these *cases interfere with* your health. When did you last eat today?"

"Probably at breakfast," Hudson *admitted*.

"You see. You need your energy," Miss Paddington said in a motherly tone.

"What I need is a *discreet* way to *investigate* the death of Sir Anthony Baker," Hudson *mumbled*.

"Maybe that nice Elvira Elliot can help you. She phoned earlier today."
This immediately *lifted* Hudson's *spirits*. "Did she say what she wanted?"

ÜBUNG 19 !

Übung 19: Ordnen Sie die Satzhälften richtig zu!

1. ☐ These cases should not
2. ☐ You can do more thinking
3. ☐ I was just thinking
4. ☐ I wish I had been
5. ☐ He needs a discreet
6. ☐ He admitted
7. ☐ You need
8. ☐ The news lifted

a) able to talk to him.
b) his spirits.
c) way to investigate the case.
d) your energy.
e) over dinner.
f) interfere with your health.
g) out loud.
h) that she was right.

"She *mentioned* an *insurance policy*. She tried to *reach* you on your mobile phone, but couldn't. You're to call her back."
"My mobile? Ah yes, I put in on silent while I was at Sir Reginald's London club. I hope no one else has tried to *reach* me."
Hudson looked at his mobile phone. The display showed that he only had one missed call.
"Miss Paddington, please keep my dinner warm until I get off the phone."
Miss Paddington smiled and left the room.
I wonder what *insurance policy* Elvira wants to talk about, Hudson thought as he waited for her to answer the phone. After a few rings, he heard her voice on the other end of the *line*.
"Elvira! I'm surprised you are able to take my call on a Saturday evening!" the inspector joked.

"There's no need to worry about my social life. I'm going out later."
Hudson *frowned* and *grunted* something.
"What was that?" Elvira asked.
She seemed to be amused.
"Nothing. I'm returning your call. Miss Paddington said you wanted to talk to me about an *insurance policy*."
"That's right. Sir Anthony Baker's *insurance policy* actually. His son called the *insurance claims* hotline and *inquired* about *cashing in*."
"That was fast. Sir Anthony just died this afternoon."
"The same thought *crossed the mind* of the person who *handles* Sir Anthony's *insurance policy*," Elvira continued. "He called me and asked me to look into the *case*. Did Sir Anthony really *die of natural causes*?"
"It's funny that you should ask," Hudson replied.
"Should I take that as a 'no'?"
"I'm glad you're not a reporter, Elvira. I don't have to worry about you *quoting* me. Let's just say that I don't think you should start paying *insurance premiums* right away."
Hudson paused. Miss Paddington's words *echoed* in his mind. Maybe Elvira could help.
"I have an idea. I'm going to visit Michael and Stella Baker tomorrow. Why don't you come along?"
"*Count me in!* What time?" Elvira Elliot asked.
"I wouldn't want to get you up too early after your big date tonight," Hudson said sarcastically.
"I'll pick you up at nine o'clock, sharp," she said, ignoring his comment. "And James?"
"Yes?"
"Tell Miss Paddington that I would love to have one of her *delicious scones* for breakfast."

ÜBUNG 20 !

Übung 20: Ordnen Sie die Beschreibungen der richtigen Person zu!

1. ☐	This person is Inspector Hudson's boss.	a) John
2. ☐	This person is Sir Anthony's daughter.	b) Miss Paddington
3. ☐	This person is Finmore's wife.	c) Sir Reginald
4. ☐	This person is the victim.	d) Tony Barrington
5. ☐	This person was Michael's brother.	e) Bonnie
6. ☐	This person works for James Hudson.	f) Sir Anthony
7. ☐	This person is a forensics genius.	g) Stella

Chapter 3: Family Ties

The doorbell rang at exactly nine o'clock on Sunday morning. Miss Paddington *smoothed* her *apron* and opened the door to Elvira Elliot, who was waiting *patiently* on the other side. Her long red hair fell naturally over one shoulder.

"Good morning, Miss Elliot," Miss Paddington said.

"Good morning, Miss Paddington," Elvira replied smiling. "Mmm, can I smell fresh *scones*?"

"You certainly can!" Miss Paddington said *proudly*. "Come in."

"Thank you, Miss Paddington, but I don't know if we have time to eat here. Can I take some with me?"

"My *scones* are not meant to be eaten in a car. You and Inspector Hudson will eat a *proper* breakfast before you start working."

ÜBUNG 21 !

Übung 21: Unterstreichen Sie die richtige Variante der Verbformen!

1. My scones are not mean/meant to be eaten in the car.
2. I usually prepare/am preparing scones in the morning.

3. Miss Paddington's words echoed/are echoing in his mind.
4. You should not paid/pay the insurance premium yet.
5. If you bear with me/will bear with me, I'll tell you what I'm thinking.
6. I love/am loving her scones.
7. I was putting/put my phone on silent when I was in the club.
8. Elvira waited/was waiting patiently at the door.

Ten minutes later, Inspector Hudson found Elvira and Miss Paddington talking at the kitchen table. Both women looked up as he walked in. Miss Paddington pointed to the *scones* and *clotted cream* on the table.

"Your *scones* are waiting for you, Inspector," she said as she rose.

Hudson *glanced* at his watch. "Maybe I can take mine with me. We really have to be going."

"If you were in such a hurry, you would have opened the door for me at nine o'clock. I think you have time to eat a *scone*. Michael Baker isn't going to leave the country before we talk to him. He needs the *insurance* money," Elvira said.

Hudson sat down. "I can't argue with that logic."

"You may not find Michael Baker at his home anyway," Miss Paddington said.

Hudson looked at Miss Paddington surprised. "Why not?"

"He has some things to do at his father's *mansion* today."

"Really?" Hudson asked.

"That's what Hannah said last night," Miss Paddington replied.

Elvira took the last bite of her *scone*.

"Who's Hannah?" she asked.

"Hannah is Michael's housekeeper," Miss Paddington said. "She's a friend of mine and called me last night. It seems as if Michael is very *anxious* to *settle* some financial *affairs*."

ÜBUNG 22 !

Übung 22: Welches Wort ist das „schwarze Schaf"? Unterstreichen Sie das nicht in die Reihe passende Wort!

1. hurry, delay, speed, fast
2. expect, shock, surprise, astonish
3. looks like, seems, it is, appears
4. clotted cream, proper, scone, jam
5. apron, kitchen, oven, coat
6. late, punctual, on time, on schedule
7. matters, business, affairs, figures

"Which *affairs*?" Hudson asked Miss Paddington.

"Hannah wasn't very specific," the housekeeper replied. "She just said that Michael seemed to be a bit nervous. I can call her and see where he is, if you want."

"That would be helpful, Miss Paddington."

"He's probably looking for his father's *insurance policy*," Elvira said as soon as Miss Paddington left the room.

"Or the *will*," Hudson took a bite of his second *scone*.

Miss Paddington returned a few minutes later. "I was right. Michael just left to go to his father's house."

"Does Hannah know how Michael's sister, Stella, is taking the news of her father's death?" he *inquired* after another bite.

"Hannah said that she was taking the news well. She spoke to her for a few minutes on the phone." Miss Paddington seemed to be choosing her words carefully.

"Sounds like a very sentimental family." Elvira's words were full of irony.

Hudson finished his *scone* and rose from the table.

"We'll see how sentimental the Bakers are soon enough. And by the way, Miss Paddington, the *scones* were excellent."

Übung 23: Lesen Sie weiter und bringen Sie den folgenden Absatz in die richtige Reihenfolge!

1. He wished that he had not eaten so many scones.
2. Elvira laughed and looked at Inspector Hudson.
3. Elvira's red hair flowed freely as she drove her *convertible*.
4. "We're not going to put out a fire," he *yelled*.
5. Sitting next to her, Inspector Hudson held on to the door handle tightly as she turned a corner.
6. "It's much better riding in my *convertible* on a lovely day like today then in your old Bentley."

Lösung: _ _ _ _ _ _

"Keep your eyes on the road," he shouted as the car went round a curve.
"You know you love the excitement I bring to your life," Elvira joked.
Secretly, Hudson had often thought that he and Elvira made a good team. They had *solved* several big *cases* together and worked well with each other. Both Sir Reginald and Miss Paddington often *hinted* that maybe there was a bit of romance in the air as well. Hudson looked at Elvira as she sat *confidently* behind the wheel. He could understand why people thought they would make a good couple. She was attractive…
"Anyway, what do you know about Michael Baker?" Elvira asked.
Hudson was happy to answer her question. He did not want to focus on her *good looks* for too long.
"He *had a fight* with his father in public at Epsom Downs just hours before Sir Anthony's death."
"That's all?" Elvira remarked.

"I know it doesn't sound like much. But put that together with the fact that someone was with Sir Anthony before, or possibly as he died and the fight *raises questions*."

"What did they fight about?"

"Something about the family business."

"That makes sense," Elvira said. "*Rumour has it* that Sir Anthony was going to sell the company. Michael Baker was against it."

"Interesting."

"We're here," Elvira *announced*, *braking* suddenly.

ÜBUNG 24 !

Übung 24: Wählen Sie die passende Redewendung und versuchen Sie damit den Satz sinnvoll umzuformulieren!
(die from natural causes, count me in, rumour has it, cross my mind, live up to his expectations, foul play, cash in)

1. People are saying that Michael expects to get a lot of money from his father.

____

2. You can include me in your plans.

____

3. He died because he was killed.

____

4. I had the same thought.

____

5. He wants to collect the money from the insurance policy.

6. I think he was murdered.

7. Michael never did what his father hoped he would do.

The two investigators got out of the car and walked towards the house. Inspector Hudson rang the bell. It did not take long for Finmore to answer the door.

"Good morning, Finmore," Hudson said.

"Good morning, sir," Finmore replied surprisingly politely. He looked at Elvira and *raised* his eyebrow. "Another inspector to ask us questions?"

"Elvira Elliot," Elvira introduced herself. "We're here to talk to Mr Baker. Michael Baker, that is."

Finmore let them in.

"You'll find him in Sir Anthony's library. You know the way," he said to Inspector Hudson.

He left them standing in the hall.

"Strange man," Elvira said. "He's clearly the butler, but he didn't even *announce* us."

"I think he's in semi-*retirement*."

"Would you care to explain that?"

"The house is still his responsibility, but he doesn't work for Michael Baker. He doesn't have a very good opinion of him. The library is this way."

Hudson and Elvira walked down the hall.

ÜBUNG 25 !

Übung 25: Lesen Sie weiter und unterstreichen Sie die jeweils richtige Variante!

The library door was not (1.) completely/complete closed. Elvira was (2.) almost/about to knock on the door when Hudson stopped her. He pointed through the opening. Michael was (3.) sat/sitting at the desk. He seemed to be (4.) looking/look for something in the *drawers*.

"I *bet* he's looking (5.) at/for the *insurance policy*," Elvira *whispered*.

"He certainly seems to (6.) think/thinking something important is (7.) in/on one of those *drawers*," Hudson replied.

Instead of knocking on the door, he pushed it open. Michael quickly closed the *drawer* he had been looking in. He rose.

"Who are you? What are you doing here?" he asked.

"I'm Inspector James Hudson from Scotland Yard. This is Elvira Elliot. I understand that this may be a sad time for you, but we would like to ask you a few questions."

"About what?"

"The events of yesterday afternoon."

"If you're talking about my father's death, I don't know why you have to ask me questions. Sir Reginald said that my father had a heart attack."

"He did. However, there are a few questions about what happened in the minutes before your father's heart attack."

Michael Baker moved away from the desk. He offered the two investigators a seat. "I still don't see why you have to talk to me, but what do you want to know?"

"Where were you yesterday at three o'clock?" Hudson asked after everyone had sat down.

"At home. Why?" Michael Baker asked.
"Do you have any *witnesses*?"
"Do I need *witnesses* to say that I was in my own home?"
"In this *case* it would be helpful," Hudson answered.

Übung 26: Welche Wörter gehören zusammen? Ordnen Sie zu!

ÜBUNG 26 !

1. ☐ rumour	a) policy
2. ☐ good	b) questions
3. ☐ raises	c) has it
4. ☐ semi-	d) me in
5. ☐ insurance	e) looks
6. ☐ financial	f) retirement
7. ☐ count	g) affairs

"No, I was alone," Michael Baker said.
"Were you home, alone, all day?"
"What if I was?"
"Would you please answer the question?" Hudson tried to hide his *irritation*.
"I probably went out."
"Probably?" Hudson repeated, *raising* one eyebrow.
"Okay. I went out. Is that a crime?"
"It depends on what you did while you were out," Hudson replied.
"Now, I'll ask you again, Mr Baker. Where were you yesterday during the earlier part of the day?"
"Nowhere in *particular*," Michael answered.
"We have *witnesses* who say that you were somewhere *particular*," the inspector *stated*.
Michael Baker did not answer.

Elvira spoke for the first time. "Inspector Hudson didn't introduce me *properly*. I am an *insurance* investigator. I'm sure you know that Sir Anthony's *beneficiary* is only entitled to the *insurance premium* if Sir Anthony *died of natural causes*."

"We're back to that again," Michael *sighed*. "My father had a heart attack."

"After fighting with you at Epsom Downs Golf Club," Hudson added.

"My father was alive and well when I last saw him," Michael Baker said.

"And where was that?"

"At Epsom Downs. Look, I know how it must seem," Michael explained. "I *admit* it – I was angry with my father. He was planning to sell the family business. He *claimed* that Stella and I weren't good enough to keep it going after his death. *According to him*, now was the time to sell and *cash in* before everything he had built *went down the drain*."

"And you didn't agree," Hudson *concluded*.

"Hell no. That's all I've heard ever since my older brother John died. Stella and I weren't good enough to do anything. It wasn't as bad when my mother was still alive, but once she died it was as if my father was the only *surviving* family *member*. He said that his life was cursed."

Suddenly a figure *appeared* at the library door. Both Elvira and Hudson *jumped*.

"I'm sorry to have *startled you*." Hudson recognized Bonnie. "I thought you might like some tea."

She placed a *tray* on the coffee table.

"Thank you, Bonnie," Michael paused.

Bonnie did not give him a friendly look. The housekeeper left as quietly as she had *appeared*.

Übung 27: Ordnen Sie die Satzhälfen richtig zu!

1. ☐ Everything he built may
2. ☐ He is not entitled
3. ☐ You need a witness
4. ☐ The conflicting information
5. ☐ She couldn't hide
6. ☐ His son is the
7. ☐ He was nowhere

a) beneficiary.
b) her irritation.
c) to the insurance premium.
d) in particular.
e) raises questions.
f) to prove you were home.
g) go down the drain.

Inspector Hudson watched her leave. I wonder what will happen to Bonnie and Finmore now that Sir Anthony is dead, he thought. They definitely didn't have a motive to kill Sir Anthony if they are now going to be out of work. On the other hand, they were looking forward to *retiring*.

"You were telling us about a *curse*," Elvira said with interest.

"There's nothing to it, of course. Just an old man talking nonsense."

"What did he think caused this *curse*?" Elvira asked.

Michael *shrugged* and *poured* himself a cup of tea.

"Past actions. That's all he would say. Tea?" he asked coldly.

Hudson and Elvira smiled at each other.

"Yes, thank you," they said *in unison*.

As Michael *poured* the two cups of tea, Inspector Hudson watched his hands carefully. They were shaking slightly.

"Tell me more about the fight with your father yesterday. Why did you decide to fight with him at the golf club?"

"I didn't decide to fight with him there. It just happened that way. I wanted to talk to father on Saturday. I felt we needed a family meeting, but he *refused* to meet with us. The more I thought about it, the angrier I became. I *admit* that the golf club wasn't the best place to talk to him, but I didn't think he would behave the way he did."

"When was the company to be sold?" Hudson asked.

"From what I understand, they were still discussing it. But they were about to *reach an agreement*."

"That's why you wanted to speak to him during the weekend," Elvira said.

"That's right. I had to do something. I couldn't let him take my *inheritance* away from me."

"Why do you think that you are the one who will *inherit* the company?" Elvira *inquired*.

"Who else would he leave it to?"

"Maybe your sister, Stella," Elvira *stated*.

ÜBUNG 28 !

Übung 28: Setzen die richtige Zukunftsform ***will****, oder* ***is/are going to*** *ein!*

1. It's getting late. I think I _______________ go home now.
2. Inspector Hudson _______________ talk to Stella later today.
3. Oh no! I think Elvira _______________ hit that car!
4. Sir Anthony's funeral _______________ take place on Tuesday.
5. He doesn't have time today. He _______________ talk to her tomorrow.
6. I guess Hudson and Elvira _______________ talk to Michael Baker.
7. I'm sure he _______________ be able to solve the case.

Michael laughed. "You must be joking! Father was right about Stella. She has no business sense. She wouldn't know what to do with the family business. She'll be happy as long as she gets enough money to continue to *appear* in the *society pages*."
"What did your father's *employees* think about the possible sale?"
Michael *glared* at Hudson. "How would I know?"
"Don't you work there?" Elvira *exclaimed*.
Michael looked shocked. "Work there? Oh Lord, no. I stop by from time to time."
"I'm sure the *employees* are looking forward to the possibility of you taking over the company," Hudson said sarcastically.

Übung 29: Ordnen Sie die Gegenteile richtig zu!

ÜBUNG 29 !

1. ☐ in unison	a) lower
2. ☐ employee	b) start working
3. ☐ retire	c) separately
4. ☐ refuse	d) state
5. ☐ raise	e) employer
6. ☐ reveal	f) accept
7. ☐ inquire	g) hide

Michael *raised* his hand and hit the table, making the teacups *rattle*.
"Look, I don't care what they think. I can lead the company and that's what I plan to do. I'll show them all."
Hudson rose. "That's all for now, Mr Baker. Please don't make any plans to leave London until the *investigation* is over."
"What! Do you really think that the little argument I had with my father at the Epsom Golf Club caused his death?"

"No. It's what happened afterwards that we are interested in. Thank you for the tea."
Hudson walked away before Michael had a chance to reply. Elvira followed him.

ÜBUNG 30

Übung 30: Setzen Sie die richtige Präposition ein!
(about, at (2x), by, for, in, of, towards)

As the two investigators walked (1.) ____________ the car, Elvira turned to look back (2.) ____________ the *mansion*.

"Money certainly doesn't buy happiness," she remarked.

Hudson had to agree with her. "It doesn't seem to be the *case* (3.) ____________ this family."

"Do you think he loved his father?"

"Maybe he did (4.) ____________ one time," Hudson answered.

"He certainly doesn't seem to think much (5.) ________ his sister's abilities."

"It'll be interesting to find out more (6.) ____________ the family business."

"I think I can help you there. Are you looking (7.) ____________ anything specific?"

"You can start (8.) _______ finding out who this potential buyer is," Hudson *suggested*.

"Or was," Elvira added. "Michael Baker seems to think that it is his company now."
"But remember: the *will* hasn't been read yet."
"And we only have Michael Baker's word that the deal hasn't been signed," Elvira said excitedly.
A thought suddenly *crossed* Inspector Hudson's *mind*. "Could this mysterious buyer have *paid* Sir Anthony *a visit* on Saturday afternoon?"
"And maybe the two of them had an argument," Elvira *suggested*. "Maybe something has gone wrong with *terms and conditions* of the sale?"
"Sir Anthony could even have *changed his mind*."
"Something that Michael said could have made Sir Anthony believe that Michael was fit to run the company after all." There was *doubt* in Hudson's voice.
"You never know. They were family, after all."
"That's the problem with this *case*."
"Why is that a problem? Murders often happen within families," Elvira said.

Übung 31: Welches Wort ist das „schwarze Schaf"? Unterstreichen Sie das nicht in die Reihe passende Wort!

1. terms, contract, conditions, murder
2. insurance, policy, beneficiary, brewery
3. will, bill, beneficiary, inherit
4. family, enemies, friends, relatives
5. crying, smiling, joking, laughing
6. foul play, murder, natural causes, killing
7. marriage, engagement, divorce, honeymoon

"Yes, I know, Elvira. That's not what I meant," Hudson explained. "The problem is that I feel as if there is a lot that I don't know. I don't know the identity of the mysterious buyer. I don't know if Michael visited his father on Saturday afternoon around three o'clock. I don't even know if someone was with Sir Anthony when he died."

Elvira nodded. "I see what you mean. There are a lot of unanswered questions."

"Yes, but there is one thing I do know," Hudson *announced* suddenly.

"What's that?"

"We aren't going to get any answers standing here talking. It's time to *pay* Stella Baker *a visit*."

The two investigators got in the car and *fastened* their seat belts.

"*Hold tight!*" Elvira said as she started the car.

"I was afraid you were going to say that," Hudson *grunted*. "Just remember: I want to stay alive long enough to *solve* this *case*."

Elvira grinned. "Relax, you're safe with me!"

! ÜBUNG 32

Übung 32: Trifft die Aussage zu? Markieren Sie mit richtig ✔ oder falsch – !

1. Inspector Hudson thinks that Elvira is a good driver. ☐
2. Inspector Hudson has all the answers to the mystery. ☐
3. Michael thinks his sister does not know much about business. ☐
4. Murders within families are common. ☐
5. Michael thinks that he is going to inherit the brewery. ☐
6. Michael is happy to answer all of Hudson's questions. ☐
7. The will has already been read. ☐
8. Sir Anthony wanted to sell the company. ☐

Chapter 4: A Mysterious Rendezvous

Stella Baker lived in an exclusive part of London. Her house was an attractive Victorian building.

"I wonder if Michael and Stella will be able to *afford* their lifestyle now that Sir Anthony is dead," Elvira said.

"Michael Baker seems to think so, now that the family business isn't being sold."

Hudson rang the doorbell. There was no answer. Elvira looked at her watch.

"It is lunchtime on a lovely Sunday. She could be out."

Inspector Hudson looked at the windows. He saw the curtain move in one of them.

"You could be right, but I don't think so."

He rang the doorbell again and then knocked on the door. "Police," he *yelled*.

Übung 33: Kreuzen Sie die richtige Definition an!

ÜBUNG 33 !

1. afford

a) ☐ cannot buy

b) ☐ able to buy

2. fasten

a) ☐ close

b) ☐ open

3. admit

a) ☐ say something is not true

b) ☐ say something is true

4. mansion

a) ☐ big country house

b) ☐ city apartment

5. Hold tight!

a) ☐ Relax!

b) ☐ Don't let go!

6. irritate

a) ☐ annoy

b) ☐ praise

7. brake

a) ☐ slow down

b) ☐ hurry up

A *prim*-looking woman opened the door.

"Yes?"

"Is Ms Stella Baker in? We would like to speak to her."

"You're from the police?" the woman asked.

Inspector Hudson showed her his *ID*. He heard footsteps inside the flat. A tall, stylishly dressed, blond woman *appeared* at the door. "Police, did you say? It's okay," she said to the *prim*-looking woman. "I'll talk to them."

"Yes, Ma'am."

The woman walked away.

"I tell her not to call me that, but she is very *old-fashioned*," Stella Baker smiled.

"And *protective* as well," Inspector Hudson said.

"You noticed, Inspector…"

"Hudson. This is Elvira Elliot."

"I'm an *insurance* investigator," Elvira explained.
"Today must be my lucky day. A police inspector and an *insurance* investigator. Oh, where are my *manners*. Come in."
Stella Baker led them to the sitting room. Several dresses were *neatly* hung over the back of a chair near a group of boxes.
"Going somewhere?" Hudson asked, looking at the dresses.
"Oh, those. No, I'm getting them ready to ship to my customers."
"Your customers?" Elvira asked.
"Yes, I'm a dress designer," Stella Baker replied. "It began as a hobby. Then I found out that I was good at it. But I'm sure you didn't come by to see my latest designs. What can I do for you?"
"We're here to ask you some questions. It's concerning your father's death," Hudson explained.

Übung 34: Lesen Sie weiter und unterstreichen Sie die richtige Variante!

ÜBUNG 34 !

"Father's death?" Stella looked at Elvira. "Does this have (1.) nothing/something to do with his *insurance* (2.) policy/police? Knowing Michael, he's already trying to *cash* (3.) on/in."
"It's (4.) relative/related," Elvira answered.
"When was the last time you saw your father?" Hudson asked.
"Last week, I think it was. Michael had wanted to (5.) hold/keep a family meeting to talk about the business this weekend. But father *refused*. Nothing was more important than his Saturday golf (6.) match/play."
"Did you think the meeting was (7.) necessary/necessity?" Hudson asked.
"No. (8.) Because of/In spite of what people think, I do not need the family money to exist. It's different for Michael. He has always

lived in the shadow of our older brother John. He's never had the courage to (9.) start/build a business on his own. The only way he has ever managed to make money is by *gambling*."

"So you agreed with the sale of the family business," Elvira *stated*. "I didn't have anything against it. I believe in protecting our family's *heritage*. Father *obviously* thought that selling the company was the way to do it."
"Your brother seems to think that he will *inherit* the company," Inspector Hudson said.
"My brother has always *counted his chickens before they're hatched*. My father's *will* hasn't been read yet."
Inspector Hudson was about to ask Stella about her brother's *gambling* when her mobile phone rang. She looked at the number.
"Excuse me, I have to answer this," she said as she rose from her chair.
"You don't have to worry. That doesn't change anything. The *delivery* will be made this afternoon," Hudson heard her say as she walked out of the room.

ÜBUNG 35 !

Übung 35: Beantworten Sie die Fragen zum Text!

1. What did Elvira and Inspector Hudson have for breakfast on Sunday morning?

____

2. How did Michael Baker make money?

____

3. What is Stella Baker's job?

4. What is Sir Reginald's relationship to the Bakers?

5. Why does Inspector Hudson think that someone was with Sir Anthony when he died?

6. Why is Stella's housekeeper not happy to see Inspector Hudson?

Elvira rose and picked up one of the dresses on the chair.
"I would wear this," she said as she held the red *silk* dress up against her body.
"*Off duty*," Hudson said.
Elvira smiled. "Of course."
She put the dress down. "Stella seems to be doing quite well for herself. Her customers even call on Sundays."
"She does seem to have more business sense than her brother." Hudson looked around. "Do you think all of this comes from her business, though?"
"I can probably *check* that out when I *do* some *research* on the family business," Elvira said.
"Sounds like a good idea."
Hudson heard footsteps *approaching* the sitting room. He put his finger to his lips. Elvira returned to her place on the sofa. A few seconds later, Stella walked into the room and smiled sweetly.

ÜBUNG 36 !

Übung 36: Ergänzen Sie die fehlenden Wörter!

1. He has a lot of money. He has a for__________.
2. She knows she is a good driver. She is con____________.
3. Miss Paddington always wears an ap________ when she cooks.
4. Inspector Hudson didn't want people to hear his mobile phone ring so he put it on sil____________.
5. They had a fight at the golf club. Michael almost att__________ his father.
6. Sir Anthony said no to a family meeting. He ref__________.

"Now where were we?" Stella Baker asked.
Even though she was smiling, Hudson could see that she was more nervous than before. Her hands moved nervously in her *lap*.
"Your father's *will*," Elvira answered.
"Oh yes, that. I don't know anything about father's *will*. I never really thought much about it."
"Never?" Hudson asked.
"I know it may sound strange, but you didn't know my father. He was very *old-fashioned*. I'm not a boy and I'm the youngest. He always expected me to find a man to take care of my needs." Stella laughed. "Marrying my father may have been the only way my mother could achieve financial stability, but things are different these days. I chose to take care of myself."
"Did you start your business without you father's help, Ms Baker?" Elvira *inquired*.

Übung 37: Was ist gemeint? Finden Sie den passenden Begriff!

ÜBUNG 37 !

1. when someone comes towards you, they: __________

2. a policeman who is not working is: __________

3. a delicate, soft type of cloth is: __________

4. to risk money is to: __________

5. when things are tidy and in place, they are: __________

6. formal and carefully correct behaviour is: __________

"I *inherited* some money from my mother. Father has given me money from time to time, but I didn't use it for my business."

Hudson remembered Michael's words about Stella. It was a bit ironic that she used her mother's money for business *purposes* and her father's to *support* a *lavish* lifestyle.

"Your brother didn't seem to know much about the people who worked for your father," he said.

"What would you like to know about them?" Stella asked.

"How did they feel about the possible sale of the company?"

Stella *frowned*. "I can't say how they felt about the sale, but I'm sure they'd do anything to keep my brother's hands off of the company."

"That sounds rather drastic," Elvira said.

"I don't know what Michael told you, but even if he does *inherit* the company, I'm sure he has no plans to run it."

"What do you mean?" Inspector Hudson asked.

"Even though my brother loves money, he hates work. Father was right about him. John had all of the business sense. Michael could never *successfully* run a company. I could do it much better."

Hudson heard *jealousy* in her voice.

"Please continue," he said after a short pause.
"Michael will sell the company as well, of course," she said.
"So it will be sold *no matter who* controls it," Elvira said.
"But there's a difference. I'm sure my father wanted to sell it to someone who would look after it. Michael won't care who he sells it to. The only thing that means anything to him is money."
Stella's tone had become aggressive.

ÜBUNG 38 !

Übung 38: Übersetzen Sie die Sätze ins Deutsche!

1. She is jealous of her brother.

....

2. He inherited money from his father.

....

3. Sir Anthony wants the brewery to be looked after.

....

4. Michael Baker shouldn't count his chickens before they are hatched.

....

5. She has a lavish lifestyle.

....

6. He doesn't have any business sense.

....

"Do you know anyone at the company who could tell us a bit more?" Hudson asked.
"I can give you a few names," Stella said. "Adam Jones, Daphne Edwards, and Peter Johnson. They should be able to help you."
Stella looked at her watch. "Are we almost done? I don't want to be rude, but I promised my customer that I would *deliver* a dress in half an hour. She needs it for a special event tonight."
"I just have one more question," Hudson said. "Where were you yesterday at 3:00 p.m.?"
Stella looked shocked.
"Here. I had a customer. Do I need to give you her name?"
"Not at the moment, but we may ask for it later. Thank you, Ms Baker. That's all for now," Hudson said.

Hudson got into Elvira's car and shut the car door.
"She didn't seem to be very upset about her father's death, did she?" he asked Elvira.
"At least she doesn't seem to be waiting to profit from it like her brother."
"That's true, but I still want you to *check* out her business."
Hudson looked at Stella's house. "Elvira, didn't Stella Baker say that she was going to *deliver* a dress?"
"Yes, she did."
"She must have forgotten it."
Elvira looked in the same direction as Inspector Hudson. Stella was getting into her car.
"She's only carrying her handbag."
"It must be a small dress. Why don't we follow her?" Hudson *suggested*. "She can't be going far. She said that her customer expected her in half and hour."
"Good idea," Elvira replied and started her car.

ÜBUNG 39 !

Übung 39: Setzen Sie folgenden Absatz in die Vergangenheitsform!

"Finally!" Elvira *exclaims* twenty minutes later as she brings the car to a halt. "I think I am going to fall asleep behind the wheel." Inspector Hudson laughs to himself. He knows that it must have been hard for Elvira to drive so slowly.
She and Stella Baker may share the same taste in dresses, but Stella definitely isn't a fan of high speed, Hudson thinks.

He watched Stella as she got out of the car and went to stand in front of a well-known café. It was not long before a person wearing *baggy* trousers, a light jacket and a cap *approached* her. The two people talked to each other for a few minutes. Then, Hudson saw Stella hand over something that looked like an envelope.
"What's that?" he asked Elvira.
"What?"
"Didn't you see it? Stella Baker gave something to the person she's talking to. And it definitely wasn't a piece of clothing."

Elvira *shrugged*. "It's not a crime to meet someone in a public place and give them something."

"I know," Hudson said *impatiently*. "But isn't it strange that she told us she had to meet a customer to *deliver* a dress? Did you see how nervous she was after that phone call? She's hiding something. I can feel it."

Stella and the other person started to walk in opposite directions.

"They must have finished their business, whatever it was," Elvira said. "We could always ask her about it."

"*I'd rather* find out more about the person she just met."

Hudson got out of the car. *Oncoming* cars kept him from crossing the street. A *lorry* stopped in front of him. He could no longer see the other side of the street. He tried to look around the *lorry*, but could not. By the time the *lorry* had driven away, the person had disappeared.

"Damn," he *mumbled* as he got back into the car.

"I lost him, or her," Hudson *sighed*.

"Don't worry, I saw whoever it was going around the corner. *Hold tight!*"

The car shot away from the *curb*. Hudson thought that he was going to have a heart attack as Elvira *barely* missed hitting an *oncoming lorry*. He closed his eyes.

"You aren't much help with your eyes closed," Elvira said dryly. "If you want me to keep my eyes on the road, you have to watch for that person with the hat."

"Quite right," Hudson said as he opened his eyes.

He heard a plane as it flew overhead. Richmond upon Thames was one of the most beautiful *boroughs* in London. It sat on both sides of the River Thames and was full of lovely green parks. Only the constant sound of airplanes overhead ruined the otherwise peaceful atmosphere.

Hudson looked on both sides of the street, but could not find the person he was looking for.
"Whoever it was could be anywhere by now," he *sighed*.
"I'm afraid so," Elvira agreed. "But you know who could tell us more about the mysterious rendezvous."
"*Okay, you've made your point!*" said Hudson. "Let's *pay* Stella Baker another *visit*."

ÜBUNG 40

Übung 40: Bilden Sie sinnvolle Phrasal Verbs!

1. ☐ hand	a) of
2. ☐ ask	b) into
3. ☐ profit	c) over
4. ☐ get back	d) from
5. ☐ take care	e) up
6. ☐ pick	f) for

Thirty minutes later, Inspector Hudson and Elvira were standing on Stella's doorstep, talking to the *prim* housekeeper again.
"Did you forget something?" she asked.
She was *obviously* not happy to see them back on her doorstep.
"No. We need to talk to Ms Baker again," Hudson said.
"Again?"
"That's what I said. Is she in?"
"Come in," she said.
After showing them to the sitting room, the housekeeper left them alone, closing the door behind her.
"She's being very *secretive*, isn't she?" Elvira commented.
"Stella Baker did *admit* that she was *protective*."
"Do you think that she feels she needs to protect Stella from us?"

"*Obviously*, she does," Hudson replied.
He *glanced* at the chair which held the dresses. The red dress was still on top.
"Stella definitely didn't take any of those dresses to customers."
"And those were the ones she said she had to *deliver*."

Übung 41: Setzen Sie die richtige Präposition ein!
(of, to, in, for, at, on)

ÜBUNG 41 !

1. Hudson glanced ________ the chair.
2. I would like to talk to Stella Baker. Is she ________?
3. Richmond on the Thames sits ________ both sides ________ the river.
4. He could not find the person he was looking ________.
5. We need to talk ________ you.

The door opened abruptly. Stella Baker gave Hudson and Elvira a smile that was *obviously* not real.
"You're lucky that you came back when you did. I just returned and was about to go out again."
"Then we won't keep you," Hudson said.
"Did your customer like the dress you *delivered*?" Elvira asked *innocently*.
"Yes, she loved it," Stella said nervously. "In fact, she's given me another order."
So I was right, Inspector Hudson thought. He could have *hugged* Elvira. He addressed Stella instead.

"That's funny," he said. "How could someone love something they never received?"

"I don't know what you're talking about, Inspector," Stella replied *forcefully*.

"Come now, Ms Baker. I don't think your memory is that short. Who did you meet and what was it about?" Hudson's tone was just as *forceful*.

"It's none of your business," Ms Baker *snapped*.

"I'm *conducting* a criminal *investigation*. That makes it my business."

"A criminal *investigation*. I can't believe what I'm hearing. When did meeting a friend become a crime?"

"When you decided to lie about it. Your actions could be seen as *obstruction of justice*," Elvira said.

"Exactly what crime are you *investigating*? I thought you were here because of my father's *insurance policy*."

"We have reason to believe that someone was with your father when he had his heart attack," Hudson informed Stella. "That person may have let your father die or even *intentionally* angered him in the hope that he would have a heart attack."

ÜBUNG 42 !

Übung 42: Ordnen Sie die Synonyme zu!

1. ☐ secret	a) on purpose
2. ☐ hug	b) clearly
3. ☐ intentionally	c) prefer
4. ☐ snap	d) embrace
5. ☐ protect	e) hidden
6. ☐ rather	f) guard
7. ☐ obviously	g) say angrily

Stella opened her mouth as if to protest and then closed it. She looked from Elvira to Inspector Hudson.
We've got her now, Hudson thought.
"Okay. What do you want to know?" Stella asked, rather quiet now.
"Who did you meet and why did you lie to us about it?" Hudson *inquired* again.
Stella took a deep breath and said: "The person I met is *blackmailing* me."
Both Hudson and Elvira remained silent. Stella took another deep breath.
"I have a half-brother."
"Huh?" Elvira *exclaimed*.
Stella gave a *faint* smile. "That's how I felt when I found out. I couldn't believe it. Then the *blackmailer* showed me some *evidence*, though it was all quite *circumstantial*: love letters, hospital records, pictures. Even if it isn't true, I couldn't let the *blackmailer* go public with that kind of information. I had to think of the family name."
"Is the *blackmailer* your half-brother?" Elvira asked.
"No, it's someone my half-brother knows. I don't even know if it is a man or a woman. Their voice is always *disguised* on the phone and I *suppose* you saw how the person dresses. Whoever it is never speaks. I just hand over the money."

Übung 43: Lesen Sie weiter und setzen Sie das richtige Wort ein!
(rival, illegitimate, bring, world, last, temper, several

"Did you go to Sir Anthony about this?" Hudson asked.

"No! How could I? I tried (1.) ______________ times, but I just couldn't (2.) ______________ myself to ask him if he had fathered an (3.) ________________ child."

"Did you tell Michael?" Elvira asked.

"Michael would be the (4.) ______________ person I would tell. It would be too dangerous. Michael couldn't stand to have another (5.) ______________. Not even an *illegitimate* one."

"What would he do?" Elvira wanted to know.

"Michael has a violent (6.) ________________ and lots of… not very 'friendly' friends. I don't want anything bad to happen to my half-brother, I just don't want the whole (7.) ________________ to know that I have one."

"Does your half-brother know who his real father is?"
"Not *according to* the *blackmailer*. That's the deal. No one will ever know."
"How did the *blackmailer* find out without your half-brother knowing himself?" Elvira asked.
"I never thought of asking. The news was so shocking. I just wanted to *cover it up*."
"How long has it been going on?" Elvira *inquired*.
"About half a year. I remember because it started at about the time father began looking for a buyer for the company."
"When will you meet the *blackmailer* again?" Hudson asked.
"Next month."
"Can you get in contact with the person before then?"

"No. The *number* is *unlisted*. I always wait for the *blackmailer* to call me."

"He or she probably calls from a telephone box," Hudson said.

"Inspector, Miss Elliot, you won't tell anyone about this, will you?"

"We'll do our best to be *discreet*," Hudson *assured her*.

"You'll do your best!" Stella screamed. "You don't know how much money I've paid to keep this quiet. It has nothing to do with your criminal *investigation*."

"We'll be the ones to decide that," Hudson replied. "If you happen to hear from the *blackmailer* again, call me immediately. Good afternoon, Ms Baker."

Übung 44: Lesen Sie weiter und ordnen Sie die Buchstaben in Klammern zu sinnvollen Wörten!

Inspector Hudson and Elvira left the (1. sohue) ____________.

As he opened the car door, he saw Stella Baker's (2. mrpi) ____________ housekeeper running towards them.

"Inspector, Inspector." She looked around as she *approached* the car. "Inspector, I have something that may (3. terinset) ____________ you."

"What would that be?" Inspector Hudson was (4. dzpzuel) ____________.

Nervously, Stella's housekeeper *reached* into her (5. tpokce) ____________.

"Here," she said as she showed Inspector Hudson a (6. erpitcu) ________________. "This is my Ms Baker (7. tnemgei) ________________ that *dreadful* person. I knew this picture would *come in handy* some day."

"Did you take it?" Inspector Hudson asked.
"Yes. I couldn't just stand by and watch Ms Baker *suffer*. She's been terribly unhappy ever since that person started calling her. So I followed her one day. Can you identify the person?"
Hudson looked at the picture. The *blackmailer* was wearing the same pair of *baggy* trousers and the same cap.
"We'll try," he said.
To Hudson's *relief*, the drive back to his house was much calmer than his experience earlier in the day. Elvira *was deep in thought* as she drove.
"How did you know that Stella was trying to hide something?" Elvira asked Hudson.
"You learn to recognize these things in my *line of business*."
"My *line of business* isn't so different from yours," Elvira reminded him. "Too bad we couldn't find out more about the person Stella met."
"We will," Hudson *assured her*. "The picture Stella's housekeeper gave us may help."
When they arrived at Inspector Hudson's house, the two investigators agreed to meet again on Monday afternoon.
"I should be able to get some of the information you're looking for by then," Elvira said.
"I just hope I don't have to talk to Sir Reginald before then," Hudson *sighed*.

"What will you tell him if you do have to talk to him?"
"The only thing I can tell him: I have four main *suspects* in the death of one of his best friends. The *victim's offspring*, both legitimate and *illegitimate*, and a *blackmailer*."

Übung 45: Beantworten Sie die Fragen zum Text!

ÜBUNG 45 !

1. How many people does Hudson think could have killed Sir Anthony?

2. When might Elivira have more information?

3. What may help Hudson find the person who is blackmailing Stella?

4. Why did Stella's housekeeper follow Stella?

5. Who are the four main suspects in the investigation?

6. Why can't Stella call the blackmailer?

7. Who took the picture of the blackmailer?

Chapter 5: The Rebels Within

The next morning, Inspector Hudson took at deep breath as he knocked on Sir Reginald's office door. In the office, Sir Reginald put down the phone and *motioned* for Inspector Hudson to come in.

"Good morning, James. I was just about to call you."

"Good morning, sir. I thought you would want to talk to me this morning."

"I certainly do. What's this I hear about you *bothering* Michael and Stella Baker yesterday?"

"I wasn't *bothering them*, Sir Reginald. I was *conducting* a murder *investigation*."

"That doesn't mean that Sir Anthony's children have to be treated like *suspects*."

"Even if they are?"

"I've known those two since they were babies. They are not capable of murder," Sir Reginald replied *forcefully*.

"Sir, I didn't *accuse* either of them of murdering Sir Anthony. We just asked them a few questions."

"You and that nice Miss Elliot," Sir Reginald said, smiling.

"Elvira Elliot was with me. She had a few questions of her own."

Sir Reginald leaned forward. "She did, did she?"

"Yes, she did and still does. Michael Baker has already started trying to *claim* his father's life *insurance policy*."

"He has?" Sir Reginald sounded *confused*. "Why would he do that so soon?"

"Good question."

Inspector Hudson started to relax. Sir Reginald was *obviously* beginning to understand that he and Elvira had had a good reason for talking to Sir Anthony's children. He also thought that Sir

Reginald would be the perfect person to *provide* some background information about the *siblings*.

Übung 46: Markieren Sie mit richtig ✔ oder falsch – !

ÜBUNG 46 !

1. Sir Reginald does not want to talk to Hudson. ☐
2. Stella and Michael are siblings. ☐
3. Hudson accused the siblings of murdering Sir Anthony. ☐
4. Michael Baker wants to claim his father's life insurance. ☐
5. Sir Reginald has known Stella and Michael all their lives. ☐
6. Only Hudson talked to Stella and Michael. ☐

"Sir Reginald, you've known Michael and Stella Baker for a long time. Since they were babies, you said earlier. What can you tell me about them?"

Sir Reginald sat back in his chair and thought for a moment. "Michael is a wild one. Got into lots of trouble when he was younger. But you won't find any official *mention* of it anywhere," he said calmly.

Hudson understood. "It was all taken care of – *off the record*."

Sir Reginald nodded.

"Stella Baker said that Michael likes *gambling*," Hudson said.

"In more ways than one," Sir Reginald replied.

Hudson *raised* his eyebrow. "How do you mean?"

"Sex, drugs and rock n' roll. Michael likes to *live life in the fast lane*. Sometimes that gets him into trouble. *Underage* girls, married women."

"I see," Hudson said slowly.

"Sir Anthony *turned a blind eye* while John was alive. His motto was: just don't *drag* the family's name *through the mud*. But when

John died, everything changed. He tried his best to prepare Michael to take over the family business."
"But it didn't work."
"You've met Michael," Sir Reginald replied. "What do you think?"
"My guess would be that it didn't."

ÜBUNG 47

Übung 47: Bringen Sie die Wörter in die richtige Reihenfolge!

1. died everything John when changed

____

2. his said gambles sister that he

____

3. record taken the it of was off care

____

4. was eye he John blind a alive turned while

____

5. through don't good mud our drag name the

____

6. trouble he of into got lately lots has

____

Sir Reginald *sighed*. "Michael just doesn't have any business sense. He was *raised* to be the second son. That meant always being in the shadow of the first. I think he did actually try to change and thought he had changed Anthony's opinion of him."

"And then he heard about the sale of the company," Hudson *concluded*.

"*Imagine* how that made him feel."

Sir Reginald sounded as if he felt sorry for Michael.

"Angry enough to kill his father?" Hudson asked.

When Sir Reginald did not reply, Hudson decided it would be better to ask another question.

"And what about Stella Baker?"

Sir Reginald smiled. "Smart girl. Very much like her mother. Unfortunately, when Agatha died, Stella did rather *take a back seat* in her father's life."

"She seems to *resent* that fact."

"Maybe she does. But not enough to kill her father. She has a very *successful* design business and a *wealthy* boyfriend. She's doing quite well for herself."

Hudson was surprised to hear about a boyfriend.

"I knew about her design business, but not about her boyfriend. She *implied* that she was on her own."

Übung 48: Wie lauten die Wörter auf Englisch? Ordnen Sie zu!

ÜBUNG 48 !

1. ☐ eifersüchtig	a) take a back seat
2. ☐ andeuten	b) raise
3. ☐ hassen	c) resent
4. ☐ in den Hintergrund treten	d) jealous
5. ☐ erfolgreich	e) wealthy
6. ☐ wohlhabend	f) successful
7. ☐ großziehen	g) imply

"Now don't get *suspicious*, Hudson. I'm sure she didn't tell you because who she's *going out with* has nothing to do with her father's death."

Now it was Inspector Hudson's turn to smile. "But you'll tell me about him anyway, won't you?"

Sir Reginald started talking. "Seems like a nice enough *fellow*. I met him one time at the golf club and one time at a dinner party. His name is Ramsey. Nathan Ramsey."

There was something else Hudson wanted to ask Sir Reginald about. He decided that now was the time to do so.

"Do Michael and Stella *get along with each other*? I ask because there seemed to be some *sibling rivalry*."

"You *detected* that, did you? The two are not the closest. Maybe that will change with Sir Anthony's death. Stella seemed to be worried about her brother and his…," Sir Reginald *cleared his throat*, "his role in all of this."

Or maybe she's just trying to *prevent* the *investigation* from ruining the family name, Hudson thought.

"Thank you, sir. You may be interested in knowing that Elvira, I mean Miss Elliot, and I will be talking to some of the key people who work for the family business."

"That's fine. Just keep me up-to-date with your progress."

"Will do, sir."

Inspector Hudson rose from his chair.

"And James."

"Yes, sir?"

"Don't create trouble where there isn't any. Anthony could have died alone."

"Do you believe that's what happened, sir? Honestly?"

Sir Reginald stared at Hudson and took a deep breath. But before he was able to answer the question, his phone rang.

Übung 49: Lesen Sie weiter und setzen Sie die richtige Präposition ein!
(about, of, in, to, for)

ÜBUNG 49 !

A message was waiting (1.) ____________ Inspector Hudson when he returned to his desk. After reading it, he called Elvira Elliot.
"At last!" she said when she heard Hudson's voice. "I've been waiting to talk (2.) ____________ you all morning."
"I had to fill Sir Reginald (3.) ____________. He gave me some interesting information (4.) __________ Michael and Stella Baker."
"Well, I have some interesting information myself," Elvira said excitedly. "Guess who's the *beneficiary* (5.) ____________ the *insurance policy*?"

"Isn't it Michael Baker?" Hudson asked.
"No."
"Stella Baker?"
"No. You have one more guess."
Hudson was losing *patience*. "Elvira," he said slowly.
"Okay, okay. The *beneficiaries* are Bonnie and Finmore."
"Sir Anthony's housekeeper and butler?"
The news *astonished* Hudson.
"Yep," Elvira said *proudly*.
"Then why did Michael call about processing the claim?"
"Because until recently, he was the *beneficiary*. Sir Anthony updated his *insurance policy* just a few weeks ago and changed the *beneficiaries* at the same time."

"And what about Stella?" Hudson asked.

"She was never *mentioned*. Maybe he had planned to leave her something else."

"So Bonnie and Finmore had both motive and *opportunity*," Hudson said.

"If they knew about the *insurance policy*, I would say so," Elvira agreed.

"Did Sir Anthony say why he had changed the *beneficiary*?"

"His *insurance* agent said that Michael had shown once again how *irresponsible* he was. So Sir Anthony decided he wouldn't throw away his *hard-earned* money by giving it to his son."

Hudson remembered what Sir Reginald had said about Michael's *behaviour*.

! ÜBUNG 50

Übung 50: Lesen Sie weiter und unterstreichen Sie die richtige Variante!

"Have you been able to find out anything about the (1.) sale/sell of the family business?" he *inquired*.

"All *trails* lead to a holding (2.) business/company. It's (3.) bought/owned by a man named Nathan Ramsey."

"Nathan Ramsey?" Hudson asked excitedly.

"Don't tell me you've (4.) listened to/heard of him."

"What's so surprising about that?"

"He's a very *successful* (5.) businessman/chef from (6.) low/high society."

Hudson laughed. "I *admit* that Nathan Ramsey is more the type of person you would know than me. But it just so happens that he's also Stella Baker's type."

"Don't tell me she's *going out with* him," Elvira said.

"*According to* Sir Reginald, they have been a couple for quite some time now."

"So her boyfriend is the man trying to buy the family business."

"It seems as if none of the family *fortune* is going to be left to Michael. I wonder if he knows that the company could end up in his sister's hands through her boyfriend," Hudson said.

"I wonder if even Sir Anthony knew. Nathan Ramsey is a very *behind-the-scenes* businessman. Lots of deals are made *on behalf of* Mr Ramsey."

"So you're saying that Sir Anthony could have been dealing with other people and didn't even realize that Nathan Ramsey was the man behind the deal."

"Exactly," Elvira agreed. "Maybe he didn't want to leave his *fortune* to either of his children."

Übung 51: Setzen Sie ***since, for*** *oder* ***ago*** *richtig ein!*

ÜBUNG 51 !

1. Stella has not seen her father ________ last week.

2. He has been in his brother's shadow ________ years.

3. His wife died over ten years ________.

4. Two months ________ I played golf there.

5. Stella's housekeeper waited ________ hours to get that picture.

6. He hasn't spoken to his father ________ over five years.

7. I've waited ________ too long for you to tell me the truth.

8. Stella has been designing clothes ________ her mother's death.

"And maybe Stella was clever enough to find a way to get her hands on it anyway."

"But in that *case* she wouldn't want her father to die before the deal went through."

"Unless, like we said before, something went wrong with the deal. Sir Anthony's murder may not have been *premeditated*. Whoever let him die could just have been *taking advantage of* the situation. What else did you find out?" Hudson asked.

"You're quite *demanding*, aren't you!" Elvira joked. "Actually, there is something else. Another *party* is interested in buying the company."

"Oh! Who?"

"The *employees* themselves," Elvira said.

"An *employee buyout*. They would have to come up with a lot of money to do that."

"*According to* my sources, it was a real possibility."

"Would Sir Anthony have sold the company to them?" Hudson asked.

"My sources say that it was very *unlikely*. It seems as if they have a better chance now that he's dead."

"Why's that?"

"Some people believe that once it is in the hands of the *board of directors,* they will decide who is going to run the company. We won't know until the *will* is read, though."

"That could be as soon as tomorrow. Who was leading the *employee buyout* group?"

"The same people Stella *suggested* that we talk to."

"Adam Jones, Daphne Edwards, and Peter Johnson. I think it's time we *paid them a visit*," Hudson *stated*.

"I'll pick you up at eleven o'clock," Elvira said and hung up before Hudson could tell her that he would be driving.

Übung 52: Setzen Sie die richtige Variante ein!

1. She felt weak and her voice was ______________.
a) faint
b) faintly

2. You're very ______________.
a) demanded
b) demanding

3. Come on! Take ______________ of her good mood and ask her.
a) disadvantage
b) advantage

4. The family company has 500 ______________.
a) employees
b) employers

5. I wouldn't give it to him. He's very ______________.
a) irresponsible
b) responsible

6. I am writing ______________ my manager.
a) in behalf of
b) on behalf of

7. I am so happy! At last Michael has asked me to ______________ him.
a) get up with
b) go out with

The smell of beer filled the air as Inspector Hudson's Bentley *approached* the *corporate head office* of the Baker's *brewery*. Inspector Hudson recognized the area from the day before. The person he and Elvira had chased had led them here.

"You didn't tell me that the Baker's family business was a *brewery*," Hudson said, trying to sound as if he were *scolding* Elvira for not giving him information.

"You didn't ask," she answered calmly, *pretending* to *yawn*.

ÜBUNG 53

Übung 53: Welche Wörter passen zusammen? Ordnen Sie zu!

1. ☐ premeditated	a) beer
2. ☐ corporate head office	b) sleep
3. ☐ brewery	c) practical
4. ☐ yawn	d) man
5. ☐ convenient	e) surprise
6. ☐ astonish	f) planned
7. ☐ fellow	g) headquarters

"Since it's taking us so long to get there, I can *fill you in*," Elvira joked.

"You should start talking. We're almost there," Hudson answered.

"It's no secret that the *breweries* are *consolidating*. The big players in the industry are making it very hard for the small *breweries* to stay in business."

"Nathan Ramsey owns one of the large *breweries*?"

"The biggest since they have taken over an American *brewery*."

"Then possibly Sir Anthony wanted to do more than just keep the company out of Michael's and Stella's hands. Perhaps he really thought that it would not *survive* as a family-owned business."

"It's possible," Elvira agreed. "Times are hard for even the best of them."
"It's *convenient* for Stella living so close, don't you think?"
"It definitely makes the way to work much shorter."
"We're here," Hudson *announced* as he expertly, and slowly, parked the car and turned off the engine.

Übung 54: Lesen Sie weiter und bringen Sie den folgenden Absatz in die richtige Reihenfolge!

ÜBUNG 54 !

1. A receptionist greeted them at the front desk.
2. After indentifying both Elvira and himself, Inspector Hudson asked for the way to the offices of Sir Anthony, Adam Jones, Daphne Edwards, and Peter Johnson.
3. The two investigators got out of the car and entered the large brick building.
4. "You'll find them all on the fourth floor," the receptionist said. "Turn left when you get out of the lift."

Lösung: _ _ _ _

When they got off the lift, they heard two people shouting in one of the offices. Inspector Hudson recognized one of the voices as Michael's. The hallway was empty. He *motioned* for Elvira to follow him. The two investigators stood at a safe distance to keep from being seen and listened to the argument.
"I have every right to be here, Peter. And I'm not going anywhere," Michael shouted. "Unfortunately, I can't say the same for you. After the *will* is read and I've *claimed* what is mine, I'm going to throw all of you out."

"You can't do that," Peter *yelled* back.

"I can and I will! The whole lot of you. And you can tell your friends Daphne and Adam the same. I've already found your *replacements*."

"You'll pay for this, *mark my words*!" Peter shouted behind him as he stormed out of office. He *bumped into* Inspector Hudson as he walked towards the lift.

ÜBUNG 55 !

Übung 55: Beantworten Sie die Fragen zum Text!

1. What is Michael going to do to with the staff if he inherits the brewery?

2. What is Nathan Ramsey's relationship to Stella?

3. Why did Sir Anthony change the beneficiary to his insurance policy?

4. What are many of the breweries doing?

5. What does Sir Anthony's company produce?

6. Who are the beneficiaries of Sir Anthony's insurance policy?

Chapter 6: A Stop in Production

"Excuse me," Hudson said.
Peter Johnson touched Hudson's arm. "Sorry for *bumping into you*," he said.
"Are you Peter Johnson?" Hudson asked.
"Yes. Can I help you?"
"Inspector James Hudson. This is my colleague Elvira Elliot. We'd like to ask you a few questions."
"Huh? I just *bumped into you*. I haven't done anything illegal."
"Your *bumping into* me has nothing to do with this. Can we go into your office to talk?" Hudson asked calmly.
Peter Johnson looked nervous. Then he smiled.
"I probably don't have much *choice*, do I?"

Übung 56: Bringen Sie die Wörter in die richtige Reihenfolge!

1. help I can you

____?

2. few like would questions you we to a ask

____

3. have anything I not illegal done

____

4. your to go we into can talk office

____?

5. have do I choice not much

6. is colleague Miss this my Elliot

Inspector Hudson shook his head and Elvira smiled, as if to apologize for Hudson's answer.
"Follow me," Peter Johnson said *reluctantly*.
He led the two investigators into a large office.
"Take a seat," he said, pointing to two chairs in front of his desk.
Peter Johnson walked around the large, wooden desk and sat down in a leather chair behind it. Hudson watched as he quickly put an envelope in his desk *drawer*. After he had closed the *drawer*, he spoke to the two investigators.
"Look, I'm sorry for the way I talked to you in the hall. This hasn't been a very good day so far."
Hudson could see that Peter was most likely telling the truth. Even if he had not heard the end of the argument with Michael Baker, he would have been able to see that Peter Johnson was not himself. His hair was *untidy* and it looked as if he had not yet shaved.

ÜBUNG 57

Übung 57: Welche Verben und Substantive gehören zusammen?

1. ☐ solve	a) a will
2. ☐ read	b) a murder
3. ☐ inherit	c) a case
4. ☐ buyout	d) a fight
5. ☐ commit	e) a fortune
6. ☐ have	f) a company

"You probably weren't able to enjoy your weekend after hearing about Sir Anthony's death," Elvira said *sympathetically*.

"No, not really. Don't get me wrong: we all knew that the old man was going to *kick the bucket* some day, it just would have been easier if he had given us some warning – maybe spent a bit of time in hospital first. As it is, he left us with a whole load of unanswered questions."

"Like who is going to run the company," Hudson said.

"Yes. I *suppose* you heard the end of my meeting with Michael."

"It seems the two of you don't *get along*, right?" Elvira commented.

"No, we certainly don't! He's a parasite. Never done a day's work in his life. I just went in there to *offer him my condolences*. You know, out of respect for the old man. But when he started giving me orders, I just *lost my temper*."

"What kind of orders?" Hudson *inquired*.

"He wanted all sorts of financial data about the company. Told me that he needed to know how *liquid* the company is because *he's in charge* now."

"And you don't respect his authority?" Hudson asked.

Übung 58: Was ist gemeint? Finden Sie den passenden Begriff aus dem Text!

ÜBUNG 58 !

1. a lot of something: ____________

2. become very angry: ____________

3. say you're sorry about a death: ____________

4. die: ____________

5. showing sadness when others suffer: ____________

6. have a friendly relationship: ____________

7. not eager to do something: ____________

"*Good heavens*, no! I'm as good as him. Although he doesn't know that now, he will soon," Peter said angrily. He paused and took a deep breath. "What I mean is, he doesn't own this company. If he did, he would ruin it. Sir Anthony wouldn't be stupid enough to leave it to him."

"Was Michael the one who told you about Sir Anthony's death?" Elvira asked.

Peter Johnson shook his head. "No, Stella Baker did."

"Oh. Do you have a good relationship with her?" Hudson asked.

"We all have a better relationship with her than with that useless brother of hers. It doesn't really matter, though."

Hudson noticed the way in which Elvira was smiling at Peter Johnson. She doesn't have to behave as if she likes him quite so much, Hudson thought.

"Why not?" she asked.

Peter Johnson returned Elvira's smile. He leaned forward towards her.

"Because neither one of them is going to get the company," he said, looking into her eyes.

"So who is?" she asked sweetly.

"We are. The *employees*," he said *confidently*.

"You say that as if it were a fact," Hudson said.

Peter Johnson leant back in his chair. "There is no reason why it shouldn't be. We have the money. And who do you think has been running the company during the last few years?"

When neither Elvira nor Inspector Hudson answered, Peter Johnson continued.
"We have. The old man was here, but he only *approved* the decisions we made."

Übung 59: Unterstreichen Sie die richtige Variante!

ÜBUNG 59 !

"From what I've heard, there's (1.) an other/another option," Elvira said. "There (2.) are/is some who believe that small *breweries* cannot *survive* on their own. Sir Anthony may have decided to (3.) sale/sell to the holding company."
Peter Johnson *grunted*. "We don't need them. Sir Anthony knew that."
"Is (4.) this/that what he told you?" Hudson asked.
"That's certainly what he *implied* when we met with him (5.) last/next week. And we have been asked to be present at the reading of the *will*. Why else would he want us (6.) their/there?"
"Were Adam Jones and Daphne Edwards present at last (7.) week's/weak's meeting?" Hudson *inquired*.

"Of course. We talked about finance, marketing, and production. As you may or may not know, I am the Chief Financial Officer. Adam *heads* production and Daphne *heads* marketing. You haven't spoken to them yet?"
"You were the first one we *bumped into*," Hudson said.
"*Literally*," Elvira added.
"Wait a minute. Why are you here anyway?"
"We are the ones who usually ask the questions," Elvira joked.
"No. I mean it. Why are you here?" Peter Johnson *inquired*. "Has a crime been committed? Has there been *insider trading* of *stocks*?

If so, I'm *innocent*. I haven't told anyone what I just told you, Inspector."

Hudson *raised* an eyebrow. "No one?"

"Of course we've had *employee* meetings. The departments have been kept up-to-date with the situation. And I *mentioned* it to Michael this morning. Is that what all of this is about? *Insider trading*?"

"No, Mr Johnson. It's about murder."

Peter Johnson *blinked* twice and then started to laugh.

"Murder. You don't say. Whose?"

"Sir Anthony's."

"Stella said that the old man had a heart attack," Peter *exclaimed*. "But then that's just like Stella. Always protecting the family name."

! ÜBUNG 60

Übung 60: Wandeln Sie die Sätze ins Present Perfect um!

1. Someone was in this room.

____

2. Hudson searched for many criminals.

____

3. The blackmailer called back.

____

4. Stella's housekeeper saw the blackmailer.

____

5. Hudson found the murderer.

6. Michael shut the door.

A loud knock on the door interrupted the conversation. A tall, dark-haired woman entered the office before Peter Johnson could invite her in.
"Peter, we need to talk. Now," she said, looking at the inspector and Elvira.
"What's this about, Daphne? Can't you see I'm busy?"
"If these two are looking for a job, they can forget it if Michael gets his way."
"We aren't looking for a job. We're investigators," Elvira informed Daphne.
Daphne placed her hand over her mouth. "Oh no! They aren't *auditors*, are they? Is there a problem with the books? You said that everything was in good shape and that we didn't have anything to worry about."
"The books are fine. These two are *investigating* Sir Anthony's death."
"What's there to *investigate*? He had a heart attack. Happens to old people all the time. It was just a question of time if you ask me."
Peter Johnson *sighed*. "*Apparently*, Stella didn't tell us everything."
"Sounds just like Stella. News of a murder wouldn't look good on the *society pages*. I'm surprised that Michael has kept his mouth shut. He'll do anything for money. I *suppose* what I wanted to talk about will have to wait." She did not try to hide her *disappointment*. "The police are more important."

ÜBUNG 61 !

Übung 61: Sind die folgenden Aussagen korrekt? Markieren Sie mit richtig ✔ oder falsch – !

1. Peter Johnson works for a vineyard. ☐
2. The news of Sir Anthony's death surprised Daphne. ☐
3. The brewery's financial problems are being looked at. ☐
4. Stella tries to keep news about the family out of the papers. ☐
5. Michael Baker likes Daphne better than Peter. ☐
6. Sir Reginald also thinks that Sir Anthony was murdered. ☐

"Now that you're here, we would like to ask you a few questions as well," Hudson said to Daphne.

Daphne looked nervously at Peter Johnson.

"Don't worry," he said to her. "It hasn't been too much like the Spanish Inquisition yet."

Daphne sat down on the edge of Peter Johnson's desk.

"I don't know anything about Sir Anthony's death except what Stella told me," she said to Hudson and Elvira.

"You are a part of the *employee buyout*, correct?" asked Hudson.

"That's right. All of us are. Each *employee* is *contributing* a portion of the *asking price*."

"The company is worth a lot of money. How is it that you can *afford* to buy it?" Elvira *inquired*.

ÜBUNG 62 !

Übung 62: Setzen Sie die richtige Variante ein!

1. Sir Anthony was not liked ______________ others.

a) to

b) by

2. I have to figure ______________ the answer.
a) out
b) up

3. We suspect insider trading of ______________.
a) data
b) stocks

4. We would like to ask you a few questions as ______________.
a) good
b) well

5. I'll fill you ______________ later.
a) in
b) out

"People have used different means," Peter Johnson said. "Some people have *cashed in* their *stock* options. The company is worth a lot. I guess others have rich relatives who have given them money. Banks and the government will also *provide* a bit of financing."

"Sir Anthony's death certainly hasn't *benefited us*, if that's what you're thinking," Daphne said.

"She's right. We're having to move a lot faster than planned."

"But my sources told me that Sir Anthony was going to make a decision as soon as next week," Elvira said. "You were going to have to be in the position to buy the company this week anyway."

"That's what he led everyone to believe," Peter Johnson replied. "If he were still alive, we could probably have made a deal. Made a big *down payment* and then paid the rest later. Now we'll just have to come up with the *bulk* of the funds immediately."

"And you can do that?" *inquired* Elvira.

ÜBUNG 63 !

Übung 63: Bilden Sie die Pluralform!

1. wife	______	5. wish	______
2. inquiry	______	6. person	______
3. company	______	7. business	______
4. brewery	______	8. information	______

Hudson saw Peter give Daphne a quick look before answering.
"I'm sure we'll manage," he said *confidently*. "I've worked too hard to let this *opportunity* get away."
"When was the last time you saw Sir Anthony?" Hudson asked Daphne.
"Last week. I think that was the last time we all saw him. He held a meeting that we all attended."
She looked at Peter Johnson as she spoke.
"Where were the two of you last Saturday afternoon?" Hudson asked both Peter Johnson and Daphne.
Peter Johnson spoke first. "We were actually all together. Daphne and Adam came over to my place. We were discussing the *buyout*. As you said, *rumour had it* that Sir Anthony was going to make a move this week. We wanted to make sure we were prepared."
"Prepared financially?" Elvira asked.
"Prepared for a decision *in our favour*, but also if the decision went against us," Peter explained.
"What will you do if the holding company gets the *brewery*?" *inquired* Elvira.
"Most likely *give it a go* and try to work with the owners. Our company is profitable. Hopefully the holding company will see its role as a financier," said Peter.

"Investing in the *brewery* to make you more *competitive*," Elvira said.
"That's right," Peter agreed.
"And what if Michael *inherits* the company?" Hudson asked.
"We'll all quit," Daphne said in *disgust*. "Won't we?"
"Maybe not right away," Peter replied. "We may have some options. Like going to the *board of directors* and presenting our *case*. They could *back us* in an *effort* to buy the company from Michael."
"Stop *kidding yourself*, Peter. He'll only talk to the *highest bidder*."
"And that won't be you?" Hudson said.

Übung 64: Unterstreichen und verbessern Sie im folgenden Textabschnitt die acht falsch geschriebenen Wörter!

"Probably not," Daphne said. "There are plenty of companies that want hour informations. Patients and things like that. They *don't give a damn about* the actual *survival* of the company. We'll be absorbed and then throan out once they have want they want."
"And Michael will be laufing all the way to the bank," Peter aded.
"Or the casino," Daphne said.
"You don't have a very good onion of Michael Baker, do you?" Elvira asked.

1. ______________ 5. ______________

2. ______________ 6. ______________

3. ______________ 7. ______________

4. ______________ 8. ______________

ÜBUNG 64 !

"Have you met anyone who has? It's terrible having someone like him in the family," Peter said softly.

"Peter means in the corporate family," Daphne said quickly.

Hudson nodded. He knew that he wouldn't like to have Michael as a colleague or a relative.

"Where is Adam Jones? Miss Elliot and I would like to talk to him, too."

This time Hudson was sure that the two colleagues *glanced* quickly at one another before answering.

"Adam," Peter said. "I haven't seen him since Saturday. I've been busy this morning. First with Michael and now with you."

"I haven't seen him either," Daphne said. "I've been dealing with PR issues. Then I ran into Michael. I came here after talking to him."

! ÜBUNG 65

Übung 65: Setzen Sie ein: ***do*** *oder* ***make****? Achten Sie auf die korrekte Form!*

1. Yesterday, Elvira __________ some research.

2. The doctor __________ a mistake.

3. It was good __________ business with you.

4. They said they would __________ their best.

5. Ten minutes ago, Daphne __________ a phone call.

6. Sir Reginald did not know what to __________ of the case.

7. Sir Anthony's family did not __________ him happy.

"Why did you come to see Mr Johnson instead of Mr Jones?" *inquired* Hudson.

Daphne *shrugged*. "Because Michael *mentioned* that he had spoken to Peter," she answered. "It didn't really make sense to go to Adam."

"Maybe he's in now. Can you show us his office?" *inquired* Hudson.

"Of course," Daphne said.

When the two investigators and Daphne arrived at Adam Jones's office, they found the door closed. Daphne knocked. When there was no answer, she opened it. The office was empty.

"You see. He's not here yet," she said.

Hudson thought that she sounded relieved.

"Isn't that a little strange?" Elvira asked. "You and Mr Johnson rushed in this morning to take care of things. Wouldn't Mr Jones want to do the same?"

Daphne turned to Elvira. The look she gave her was not a nice one. Hudson thought she seemed different now that she was away from Peter Johnson. She seemed to be more nervous and not as cooperative.

"I don't control Adam's calendar, Miss Elliot. I'm sure that Sir Anthony's death has given us different priorities. Sir Anthony's *solicitor* and the *board* probably want to know about the company's financial position. Peter came in to be ready for any questions he might be asked. I have PR issues. Sir Anthony was still the *CEO* of the company. Adam deals with production. Maybe he thought it was more important to *pay a visit* to the *plant* before coming to his office."

"That could be," Hudson said. "We will *check* to see if he is there. If he should come here before we find him, please ask him to call me immediately."

Übung 66: Lesen Sie weiter und setzen Sie die Wörter passend ein!
(group, hall, door, seemed, either, business cards, likely)

He gave Daphne one of his (1.) ______________________. Daphne took it and placed it in her jacket pocket.

"I will. Now if you'll excuse me, I have some work to attend to."

She walked back down the (2.) ____________________ and into Peter Johnson's office. He heard the (3.) ____________________ close.

"Don't you think that it's a little strange that Adam Jones isn't here?" Elvira asked.

"You don't believe that he's at the *plant* (4.) ________________,"
Hudson replied.

"No. Do you?"

"It's possible but not (5.) __________________. Peter Johnson and Daphne Edwards are *as thick as thieves*. If Adam Jones is really part of their (6.) __________________, he would be here."

Elvira was *astonished* by what Inspector Hudson (7.) __________________ to be *suggesting*.

"Do you think they're *double-crossing* him?"
"I have the feeling that something is going on behind his back and that Peter Johnson and Daphne Edwards know something about it."
Elvira *sighed*. After a few seconds, she said, "I think we should see if

Adam Jones really is at the *plant* before we *jump to* any *conclusions*." The fourth floor was a lot busier than it had been earlier. Several company *employees* greeted the two investigators as they walked down the hall towards the lift. As they passed Peter Johnson's door again, Hudson heard two voices from inside the office. He looked around. No one seemed to be paying much attention to the actions of the two investigators. He touched Elvira's arm and *motioned* for her to stop. Trying to seem as natural as possible, they tried to hear what was being said on the other side of the door.
"I wish I were a fly on the wall so that I could hear what they're saying," Hudson *whispered*.

Übung 67: Vervollständigen Sie die Aussagen!

ÜBUNG 67 !

1. When the two investigators got out of the lift, Michael and Peter were…
a) ☐ fighting with each other.
b) ☐ reviewing the financial figures.

2. Elvira was surprised by…
a) ☐ the speed at which Inspector Hudson drove.
b) ☐ Inspector Hudson's thoughts.

3. Stella and Michael are…
a) ☐ siblings.
b) ☐ half-brother and sister.

4. Hudson thought that Peter and Daphne were…
a) ☐ as fat as thieves.
b) ☐ as thick as thieves.

5. Adam Jones was…

a) ☐ waiting for Inspector Hudson to talk to him.

b) ☐ missing from the building.

He could hear the word “money”. And then he heard Peter Johnson say something about Adam and the *plant*. Inspector Hudson tried to place his ear closer to the door. Suddenly his mobile phone rang. Elvira giggled. Hudson gave her a dark look and *reached* for his phone. Walking quickly towards the lift, he placed the phone to his ear.

“Hudson, where are you?” Inspector Hudson recognized Sir Reginald’s voice.

“I’m at Sir Anthony’s *brewery*, sir.”

“Good. You’re in the area. Get to the *plant* right away.”

“Actually, sir, we were on our way there anyway. What’s happened?”

“*Apparently* there was an accident before the *plant* opened this morning. A body has been found on the *premises*.”

“Is the *victim’s* name Adam Jones?”

“How did you know?”

“Just a *hunch*, sir. We’ll be right there.”

When he got off the phone, Inspector Hudson heard Elvira talking to Peter Johnson and Daphne.

ÜBUNG 68

Übung 68: Setzen Sie ***to*** *oder* ***too*** *ein!*

1. Hudson thinks that Elvira drives __________ fast.

2. I’ll take you __________ his office.

3. He would like __________ talk __________ her.

4. Peter said he had been working there ______ long ______ be fired.

5. Hudson wasn't ______ surprised to hear that Adam was dead.

"Inspector," Peter said as Hudson *approached* the group, "Daphne and I were just about to start our meeting. We were surprised to see that you and Miss Elliot are still here."

"Yes, we thought you were off hunting for Adam," Daphne said.

"As it turns out we don't have to hunt for him after all."

"You don't? Did he come in?" Peter asked, looking towards Adam's office.

"No, he's not here. Actually, you were right. He's been found at the *plant*."

Daphne gave Hudson and Elvira a nervous smile. "You see, I thought you would find him there."

"You don't look happy, Inspector," Peter Johnson *observed*.

"I'm not. Adam Jones won't be able to tell us much."

"And why's that?" *inquired* Peter Johnson.

"Dead men tell no tales," Hudson replied.

Daphne *shrieked*, before *fainting* into Inspector Hudson's arms.

Chapter 7: On the Wrong Track

"Daphne!" Peter shouted.

Both he and Elvira followed Inspector Hudson into Peter Johnson's office. Hudson gently placed her on the floor. Peter Johnson took off his jacket. He folded it quickly and placed it under her head.

"I'll call a doctor," Elvira said.

"You don't have to call one. We have one *on site*. I'll get him." Peter Johnson ran towards the door and out of the office.

"I'm surprised you let him leave the room," Elvira said.

"I think he is really worried about Daphne," Hudson said.
"They must have been close. Daphne really took the news hard," Elvira *whispered* looking at the *unconscious* woman.
"Either that, or she was surprised to hear that we found the body so soon," Hudson replied.
"But she's the one who told us to look in the *plant*."
"She told us to *check* to see if he was there. Not to search for his body." Hudson looked at Daphne a bit closer.
"What are you doing?" Elvira *inquired*.
"Seeing if she's really *unconscious*," Hudson said *impatiently*.
"Of course she is. Look at her."
"Good. *Do me a favour* and *keep an eye on* her for me. Let me know if she starts to wake up. There's something I want to see."
Hudson went to Peter Johnson's desk and opened the top *drawer*.
He heard Daphne *moan*.
"Hurry up," Elvira *whispered* loudly.

ÜBUNG 69

Übung 69: Setzen Sie, wenn notwendig, den richtigen unbestimmten Artikel ein!

1. They found the body ________ hour ago.
2. Inspector Hudson had never had ________ anyone faint in his arms before.
3. She needs more ________ information before she can answer the question.
4. Peter Johnson went to get ________ doctor.
5. Miss Paddington has baked ________ lots of scones.

6. Hudson was looking for ________ envelope.

7. Elvira did him ________ favour.

The envelope he was looking for was the only one in the *drawer*. Hudson opened it and took a piece of paper out. A photograph fell on the floor. Daphne *moaned* again. Elvira was *motioning* for him to move away from the desk. Hudson quickly picked up the photograph. It showed Peter Johnson with an older woman.
"She's waking up," Elvira informed him.
Quickly, Hudson pulled out his mobile phone and took a picture of the photo. Then he placed it back in the envelope. He was closing the desk *drawer* when he saw the office door beginning to open. By the time Peter Johnson and the company doctor entered the room, Hudson was on his knees next to Elvira. Daphne was trying to sit up.

Übung 70: Wie lauten die Redewendungen? Achten Sie auf die Wortstellung!

ÜBUNG 70 !

1. thick as as thieves ________

2. a go it give ________

3. the bucket kick ________

4. life in the live lane fast ________

5. a eye turn blind ________

6. the down drain go ________

7. condolences him my offer ________

"Are you okay, Daphne?" *inquired* Peter Johnson.

He got on his knees and took Daphne's hand. Hudson saw that he was *stroking* it gently.

"I'm fine," Daphne replied *faintly*.

"I'll be the one to decide that," the doctor said calmly.

Hudson helped Elvira stand up. The two investigators walked towards the door.

"Elvira, I want you to stay here with Daphne, the doctor and Peter Johnson. I'll send one of the officers up. I don't want these two to leave the building until I see what's waiting for me in the *plant*."

Hudson saw Peter Johnson *approaching* them.

"I'm going to *check* on Michael Baker," he said a little louder.

"Michael left. I saw him walk by when the three of you were in Adam's office," Peter Johnson informed the investigators.

ÜBUNG 71

Übung 71: Lesen Sie weiter und ordnen Sie die Buchstaben in Klammern zu sinnvollen Wörtern!

"Damn," Hudson (1. drmeetut) ________________.

"Look, the doctor will be (2. nidefhsi) ________________ *examining* Daphne soon. I'll take her home as soon as he says it's okay."

"I'm sorry, Mr Johnson, but I have to ask you to (3. iarmne) ________________ here (4. tluin) ________________ I return. That goes for Ms Edwards as well," Hudson (5. disa) ________________.

"I can't believe this. Surely you don't (6. knhti) ________________ that we had anything to do with Adam's (7. eadht) ____________? Look, Inspector, not only was he our friend, but he was also our production manager. How is the (8. acyopmn) ____________ going to exist without him?"

"Then *do him a favour* as a friend. You could know something that might help us find his murderer," Hudson answered.

The *plant* was on a large piece of land next to the office. Many police cars were parked outside the door. A young officer was leaning against one of the cars. He didn't look too busy. Hudson walked up to him and showed his *badge*. The officer stood up straight and smiled.

"Inspector Hudson, I'll show you where the body is."

"And after that would you go to the fourth floor of the *corporate head office* and *keep an eye on* two people for me? You'll find them there with Elvira Elliot."

"The *insurance* investigator. I've heard of her. The two of you work together a lot, don't you?"

Hudson *blushed*. "We often have *cases* that are related to each other. Now, where's the *corpse*?"

"It's this way, sir."

Hudson followed the young officer. As they walked past a small room, Hudson heard Michael Baker's voice. Hudson thanked the officer and gave him more detailed directions to Peter Johnson's office. As the young officer walked away, Hudson entered the room. He was surprised to see that Michael Baker had been talking to Sir Reginald.

"You finally made it," Sir Reginald said *impatiently* when he saw Inspector Hudson.

ÜBUNG 72

Übung 72: Welche Wörter passen inhaltlich zusammen? Ordnen Sie zu!

1. ☐ blush	a) law
2. ☐ deak	b) power
3. ☐ murder	c) red
4. ☐ unconscious	d) drawer
5. ☐ CEO	e) product
6. ☐ plant	f) question
7. ☐ solicitor	g) asleep
8. ☐ inquire	h) corpse

"Daphne Edwards, the Marketing Manager, *fainted* when she heard that Adam Jones's body had been found. Miss Elliot and I had to take care of the situation."

"Where is Miss Elliot?" Sir Reginald asked, looking around.

"She's with Peter Johnson, the CFO, and Daphne Edwards. I've sent a young officer to keep them company until I return."

"Good idea. We don't want any *suspects* to escape," Sir Reginald said.

ÜBUNG 73

Übung 73: Vervollständigen Sie die Begriffe!
(eye, bidder, board, payment, cross, back, on)

1. ________________ site

2. double ________________

3. keep an ________________ on

4. ________________ us

5. ____________________ of directors

6. highest ____________________

7. down ____________________

"Is that why you're keeping me here? Am I a *suspect*?" Michael Baker spoke for the first time since Hudson's arrival. "First he questions me about my father's death," he said pointing at Hudson, "and now you're *implying* that I had something to do with this second death."

"Michael, as I told you, it's best for you to give us your full cooperation," Sir Reginald said. "How would it look for the possible *heir* to the company to be found *sneaking away* from a *crime scene*?"

Michael folded his arms and tapped his foot on the floor *impatiently*.

"I wasn't *sneaking away*. I had finished what I came to do. How was I supposed to know that the Production Manager would get himself killed?"

"What exactly did you come here to do?" Hudson asked Michael.

"I needed to get some information for some interested investors. I asked that arrogant CFO to help me, but he *refused*. Said I wouldn't understand the *figures* anyway. I told him that I expected to have the documents I asked for on my doorstep by four o'clock this afternoon. Then, as if that wasn't enough, I had to talk to the snobby Marketing Director. She wasn't much help either."

"If you had cared more about the business in the past, they would have been more helpful," Sir Reginald *scolded*.

"It doesn't matter anyway," Michael Baker said. "As soon as the *will* is read and I am the legal owner of this company, I'm going to throw them all out."

"Is that what you told Adam Jones?" *inquired* Hudson.
"That's what I told the other two," Michael Baker replied. "I never spoke to Adam Jones."
"Why not?"
"I had no reason to. I needed *figures*, business plans. He just runs production."
"I'm glad you didn't talk to him with that attitude," Sir Reginald said.
"If you weren't planning to talk to him, what brought you here… to the *plant*?" asked Hudson.
"I didn't come here *voluntarily*. I was walking to my car when Uncle Reggie saw me and told me what had happened. He advised me to wait for you."
Hudson smiled when he heard Michael Baker call Sir Reginald 'Uncle Reggie'. The look on Sir Reginald's face showed that he did indeed care for the *well-being* of Sir Anthony's children.
"I don't think we have any further questions for Michael, do we, Hudson?" Sir Reginald asked.

ÜBUNG 74 !

Übung 74: Lesen Sie weiter und unterstreichen Sie jeweils die richtige Variante!

"No, that's all (1.) four/for now."
Sir Reginald gave Michael Baker a *stern* look. Michael *raised* his hand.
"I know. I know," he said. "Don't leave the country until the *case* is *solved*, (2.) right/write?"
"Michael, this is *serious*," Sir Reginald *scolded*.
"Sorry, Uncle. You don't have to (3.) worry/sorry. I'm not going (4.) somewhere/anywhere. I have to be present at the reading of the

will, (5.) remind me/remember? Goodbye Inspector Hudson, Uncle."

The two men watched as Michael (6.) left/right the room.

"What do you think?" Hudson asked Sir Reginald.

"About Michael? I don't think he had (7.) nothing/anything to do with the death of Adam Jones. He didn't even know who he was when he saw the body."

"Interesting," Hudson commented. "Where is the body, (8.) by/on the way?"

"It's hidden behind some beer *barrels*. Whoever killed him tried to make it look like an accident. Over here."

The two men walked out of the room towards a group of *barrels neatly stacked* on top of each other with the exception of about six at the end of the *row*.

"Let me guess. The killer tried to make it look like some *barrels* fell over and hit him on the head?"

"Exactly right."

"I am *assuming* Tony Barrington says otherwise," Hudson remarked.

As if in answer, Tony Barrington's head *appeared* from behind the *barrels*.

"I certainly do," the *forensics* expert said.

He pointed to the body. Hudson was *astonished* to see that the *victim* was wearing a *baggy* jogging suit. A baseball cap was at his side.

"So what killed him?" *inquired* Hudson.

He bent over and studied the body.

"Someone hit him on the head with a *blunt* instrument," Tony Barrington explained. "They knocked the *barrels* over afterwards, I would say. One hit him on the head here," he pointed to an area

on Adam Jones's head, "but that was not the *blow* that killed him."
"What's this?" Hudson suddenly asked.

ÜBUNG 75

Übung 75: Lesen Sie weiter und setzen Sie die richtigen Präpositionen ein!

Hudson pulled an envelope (1.) ________ of Adam Jones's pocket.

He looked (2.) ________ it closely.

"It's an empty envelope," Sir Reginald said, *stating* the obvious.

"Does that mean something (3.) ________ you?"

Hudson stood (4.) ________. "There's something I think you should

know (5.) ________________ Stella, Sir Reginald."

Tony Barrington pushed his glasses (6.) ________ on his nose.

"I'll leave you two alone," he said.

"No, you can stay. What I have to say is official police business

now. Stella Baker has been paying (7.) ________ a *blackmailer*."

"What!" Sir Reginald *exclaimed*. "Stella is being *blackmailed*? Why?"
"Sir Anthony had an *illegitimate* child. At least that's what the *blackmailer* claims."
"An *illegitimate* child? Anthony? I can't believe that he managed to keep something like that hidden."
"Is the *blackmailer* the *illegitimate* child?" Tony Barrington asked.

"*According to* the *blackmailer*, no."
"That's quite *disturbing* news, James, but what does Adam Jones's death have to do with Stella's situation?" *inquired* Sir Reginald.
"Stella Baker met the *blackmailer* yesterday. Elvira Elliot and I followed her. We saw her hand the person an envelope. We chased the person, but lost whoever it was. They met not far from her house and she lives near here."
"I still don't see the connection between Adam Jones's death and the *blackmailer*," Sir Reginald said.
"The person who met Stella Baker was wearing a *baggy* jogging suit and a baseball cap."

Übung 76: Was ist gemeint? Finden Sie den passenden Begriff zu den Definitionen!

ÜBUNG 76 !

1. if something is not sharp it is: ______________
2. news that upsets you is: ______________
3. when one book is on top of other books they are: ______________
4. the reason someone kills another person is a: ______________
5. when someone does something of their own free will: ______________
6. beer is produced in a: ______________
7. another word for number is: ______________

Three sets of eyes fell upon the body of Adam Jones.

"Now I see," Sir Reginald said *thoughtfully*. "James, I want you to be the one to talk to Stella. Collect Miss Elliot and go over there straight away. We'll talk to the CFO and the Marketing Director."

"Yes, sir," replied Hudson.

"And men…"

"Yes?" Hudson and Barrington replied at the same time.

"Until we know more, Adam Jones's death was an unfortunate accident."

"I can't believe that Stella Baker killed Adam Jones," Elvira *exclaimed* as Hudson drove to Stella's flat.

"Me neither. Unfortunately, at the moment the *evidence* points to her."

"When would she have killed him, though? We chased the *blackmailer* and then we lost him. When we *reached* Stella's flat, she was there."

"She could have met him again later. Or she could have been tired of having to pay him every month and got someone else to kill him. Remember, she didn't know that we were following her. Everything could have already been planned," Hudson replied *thoughtfully*.

"If she did kill him or had him killed, why would she do it so soon after the death of her father?"

"Good question. And why leave the body to be found on the ground of her family's company? If you ask me, someone is trying to *frame her*."

"You mean someone wants us to think that she killed him?" Elvira asked.

"That's what I think," Hudson replied. "But we won't know for sure until we talk to her."

*Übung 77: Ergänzen Sie die Sätze mit **any** oder **some**!*

ÜBUNG 77 !

1. Stella had to deliver ____________ dresses.
2. Elvira did research to find __________ information for Inspector Hudson.
3. Sir Reginald did not have ____________ idea who would want to kill his friend.
4. Michael did not have ____________ luck with business.
5. It will take ____________ time to solve this case.
6. There are ____________ suspects we need to talk to.
7. The case is going to be closed up ____________ day now.

Five minutes later, Stella Baker's *prim*-looking housekeeper opened the door even before Inspector Hudson rang the doorbell. Hudson thought that she seemed to be friendlier than before.
"Have you found the *blackmailer*?" she *inquired* as she let them into the flat.
"Possibly," Hudson answered.
"What a *relief* that will be to Ms Baker. She is with her *fiancé* at the moment. They are making the final arrangements for the *funeral*. It will be tomorrow morning, you know. And the reading of the *will* is going to take place in the afternoon."
"The reading of the *will* is going to take place on the same day as the *funeral*?" *inquired* Elvira.
Stella Baker's housekeeper put her hand on her *chest*. "I was also quite shocked to hear that," she *exclaimed*. "Out of respect to Sir

Anthony, I thought that they would have waited until the next day at least."

"Who wants the *will* to be read so soon?" Hudson asked.

"Sir Anthony's *solicitor* does. He says the testament *states* who will take over the company, so it needs to be read as soon as possible."

"And what about Sir Anthony's plans to sell the company?" Elvira asked.

ÜBUNG 78 !

Übung 78: Lesen Sie weiter und setzen Sie jeweils die passende Verbform ein!

"I only know what Ms Baker has (1. tell) ______________ me, but it seems as if Sir Anthony (2. make) ______________ arrangements in case he (3. die) ______________ before the sale of the company (4. take) ______________ place. He was aware of his health problems and wanted to make sure his last wishes were honoured, *no matter what*."

"He was a strong character," Elvira said.

"Ms Baker (5. inherit) ______________ many of his characteristics."

The housekeeper showed the two investigators to the same room they (6. be) ______________ in twice before. She closed the door behind her as she (7. leave) ______________.

Hudson and Elvira (8. sit) ______________ down.

"I don't think she would have been so friendly if she had known why we want to talk to Stella Baker," Elvira *observed*.

"Well, then it's a good thing that she didn't know."

Hudson paused and listened for footsteps outside the door. When he did not hear any, he continued to speak.

"What do you think about the fact that Stella is now *engaged*?"

"It could have been planned before," Elvira said. "Or maybe they were already *engaged* and nobody knew about it."

"Or maybe he's just taking care of business. Even if his holding company doesn't acquire the *brewery*, there's a chance that Stella Baker will at least get some percentage of the company, if not the whole thing. He wins either way."

"Spoken like a true romantic," Elvira laughed, *winking* at Hudson.

Hudson was about to reply, but heard footsteps coming. He put his finger on his lips. Elvira nodded. A few moments later, Stella walked into the room. She was followed by a tall, dark-haired man. His hand was on her shoulder, as if for *support*.

They make a nice-looking couple, Hudson thought. From the look on her face, he thought that Elvira held the same opinion.

The two investigators started to rise. Stella *motioned* for them to remain seated. She took a seat in a chair across from where Hudson and Elvira sat. Nathan Ramsey sat on the arm of the chair, his hand stayed on Stella's shoulder. Hudson noticed that he was gently massaging it.

Übung 79: Setzen Sie die richtige Variante ein!

ÜBUNG 79 !

1. Nathan Ramsey sat ________ the arm of the chair.
a) on
b) over

2. He was gently ________ Stella's shoulder.
a) messaging
b) massaging

3. They all wore black to the ________.
a) wedding
b) funeral

4. Elvira laughed and ________ at Hudson.
a) winked
b) blinked

5. They remained ________ when she entered the room.
a) seated
b) sitted

6. Stella and Nathan are ________ to be married.
a) enraged
b) engaged

7. He was ________ shocked to hear the news.
a) quite
b) quiet

"Inspector Hudson, Miss Elliot, I wish I could say that it was nice to see you again, but it seems as if you always come with *disturbing* news," Stella said after everyone had sat down again.
Hudson smiled. "Yes, I'm afraid that does seem to be the *case*."
"And why are you here now?" Nathan Ramsey asked.
From his tone it was *obvious* to Hudson that he *was accustomed to* getting what he wanted.

"Actually, we are here to talk to Ms Baker," Hudson replied.
Stella put her hand on Nathan Ramsey's leg to stop him from rising from the chair.
"It's okay," she said to Inspector Hudson. "Nathan can hear whatever it is that you have to say to me. I have nothing to hide from him."
"Nothing?" *inquired* Elvira.
Stella Baker looked up at her *fiancé* and then at the two investigators.
"Nothing," she repeated. "So tell me. What is it that you want to talk about?"
"The *blackmailer*," Hudson said.
Stella Baker took a deep breath. Nathan Ramsey *squeezed* her shoulder.
"Have you found him so soon?"
"Yes, I'm afraid we have," Hudson replied.
"There's no need to sound so *serious*," Stella Baker said. "You're bringing me good news. That is, unless the reporters find out and *spread* the news on the front pages of the morning paper."
"Scotland Yard does not *make a habit of* sharing such information with reporters," Hudson *assured* Stella Baker. "There's something you should know before you say anything else."
"What's that?" she asked.
Her tone *implied* that she was *puzzled*. Hudson, who *was accustomed to interrogating suspects*, tried not to let her *puzzled* tone *interfere with* the *purpose* of the visit.
Hudson took a deep breath and then said calmly, "Someone wearing a *baggy* jogging suit has just been found dead in the *plant* of your father's *brewery*."
"Oh!" Stella *exclaimed* and was speechless for a moment. Then she quickly *composed herself* again.

Übung 80: Setzen Sie das richtige Wort ein!

1. Stella told Inspector Hudson that he didn't need to sound so s____________.
2. It did not take long for her to c____________ herself.
3. She hoped that the reporter would not s____________ the news on the front page of the newspapers.
4. Nathan Ramsey s____________ Stella's shoulder.
5. He was a____________ to getting what he wanted.
6. She didn't understand why he was there and looked quite p____________.
7. Stella was not sad to hear that the b____________ was dead.

"How do you want me to react, Inspector? The loss of life always is *accompanied by* sadness. My emotions are mixed in this *case*. I'm sure you can understand why."
"Stella, I *suggest* you don't say anything else. *Obviously* these two *suspect* that you had something to do with the *blackmailer's* death. I'm right, aren't I?" Nathan Ramsey asked Inspector Hudson.
"*Partially*. Anyone who knew about the *blackmailer* and had Ms Baker's best interests in mind could have been involved as well," Hudson replied.
He did not take his eyes off Stella Baker's *fiancé*.
"I see," replied Nathan Ramsey.
Stella was about to speak when her mobile phone rang. She looked at the number on the display.

"Inspector, it's Michael. I've been trying to *reach* him. I need to talk to him about the *funeral* tomorrow. Can I tell him that I'll call him back?" Stella asked calmly.

Übung 81: Beantworten Sie die Fragen auf Englisch!

1. Why does Stella want to talk to her brother?

____

2. Why are Hudson and Elvira questioning Stella again?

____

3. Why does Hudson think that Adam may have been the blackmailer?

____

4. Why is the will being read so soon?

____

5. Where was Adam's body found?

____

6. What did Daphne Edwards do when she heard about Adam's death?

____

7. How does Stella feel about Adam Jones's death?

____

"You're not *under arrest*, Ms Baker. Of course you can talk to your brother."

Stella rose and walked out of the room as she answered her mobile phone. Although Inspector Hudson could hear her voice, he could not hear what she was saying. He decided that now was a good time to find out more about Nathan Ramsey.

"I hear that you and Ms Baker are *engaged*," he said.

"Yes, that's right, Inspector. We've been *going out* for a long time. I should have asked for her hand in marriage sooner, before Sir Anthony died."

"Well, there's no time like the present," Elvira said.

"Exactly," he said.

"I'm sure your relationship will be *convenient* if your company *is* not *awarded* the *brewery*," Hudson said.

"Ah, you know about that. What you don't know is that I'm ninety-nine per cent sure that my holding company will *be awarded* the *brewery*. My relationship with Stella is the *icing on the cake*, not the main *ingredient* in the deal."

"True love then," Elvira said.

"Yes. It's true love."

"Where were you last night?" Hudson asked Nathan Ramsey.

"Stella and I were together. I *proposed* last night and *stayed over*. Stella's housekeeper can *vouch for me*."

And she's another person who knew about the *blackmailer* and, thus, another *suspect*, Hudson thought.

Suddenly, Hudson heard Stella's voice from the door.

"You didn't tell me that it was Adam Jones's body found this morning, Inspector. Do you think he was the *blackmailer*?" she demanded to know.

"He was dressed in a jogging suit. There was a baseball cap near the body," Hudson informed her.

Übung 82: Unterstreichen Sie im folgenden Textabschnitt die richtige Variante!

"Is that all?" she *exclaimed* (1.) *forcefully*/forced.
"That and the fact that there was (2.) an/a empty envelope in his pocket. You (3.) were *delivering*/believing the money in an envelope," replied Hudson.
"The *blackmailer* could not possibly have (4.) been/being Adam Jones," Stella informed Inspector Hudson.
"And (5.) why/who is that?" Hudson asked.
"I knew Adam Jones. I know how he moved. The person who (6.) picked/has been picking up the money didn't move the same way."
"You'd be *astonished* what people (7.) could/can hide," Elvira said.

"You don't understand," Stella replied. "A few years ago, Adam Jones had a skiing accident. He damaged his knee. He had a *distinctive limp*. There's no way he could have hidden that."

Chapter 8: A Secret Revealed

At New Scotland Yard, Sir Reginald had been waiting *impatiently* for Inspector Hudson to return to his office. He was happy when he finally saw him standing at the door.
"James, come in. What did you find out? Is Stella still a *suspect*?"
"Probably not. At least not in the murder of Adam Jones. It seems as if he was not the *blackmailer* after all."
"How do you know that?"
"Adam Jones *limped*. The *blackmailer* doesn't. I know for myself. Miss Elliot and I chased him or her. In addition to that, both she and Nathan Ramsey, her *fiancé*, have an alibi for last night. He *pro-*

posed to her in quite a romantic way, or at least Miss Elliot thought so."
Sir Reginald smiled. "What did he do, *serenade her* from the street beneath her balcony?"

! ÜBUNG 83

Übung 83: Setzen Sie das richtige Fragewort ein!

1. ______________ is blackmailing Stella Baker?
2. ______________ body was found in the plant?
3. ______________ will the will be read?
4. ______________ will the reading take place?
5. ______________ is the will being read so soon?
6. ______________ did Stella know the blackmailer was not Adam?
7. ______________ is their alibi?

"That's exactly what he did, sir. You and Miss Elliot must have the same idea of romance. Anyway, as he *proposed* in quite a public way, the neighbours saw them together. A few even stopped by for a small party."
"An unplanned party. That's quite unlike Stella. I think this marriage will be good for her," Sir Reginald *mused*.
"What about Daphne Edwards and Peter Johnson?"
"They both seem to be quite sad and shocked by the news of Adam Jones's death. Neither of them has a solid alibi, though," Sir Reginald added. "Both said they were at home. We're *checking* with the neighbours to see if anyone can *confirm* that. We're also *checking* the workers at the *plant*."

"Always a good idea, sir," Hudson replied. "One of the workers could have argued with the *victim* and then killed him in a *fit of rage*."
"If that's the *case*, then the timing of Adam Jones's death has nothing to do with Anthony's death," Sir Reginald *concluded*.
"If that's the *case*, you're right," Hudson said *thoughtfully*.
Sir Reginald studied Inspector Hudson. "I can see that you think the deaths are related to each other."
"Yes, sir. I do. Someone wanted us to find him in that jogging suit. I'm going to find out why."

Übung 84: Bilden Sie positive Sätze!

ÜBUNG 84 !

1. Adam wasn't in the plant.

Adam was in the plant.

2. Sir Reginald doesn't know the identity of the woman in the picture.

3. Nobody knew that Stella was being blackmailed.

4. Elvira doesn't like Inspector Hudson's Bentley.

5. Sir Anthony didn't find his pills.

6. Michael Baker wasn't very clever.

7. Michael hasn't been told about his half-brother.

Hudson was about to leave his office when he received a call from Elvira Elliot.

"We have front *row* seats tomorrow at the reading of Sir Anthony's *will*," she told Hudson *proudly*.

Inspector Hudson was quite *impressed*. "How did you manage that?"

"I *did* some *research* and discovered that I know Sir Anthony's *solicitor*."

Elvira's contacts never *ceased* to surprise Hudson.

"So you just called him up and asked if we could attend the reading of the *will*?" he asked.

"I explained the situation to him. He won't tell me anything before the reading of the *will*, though."

"What time should we be there?"

"Two o'clock tomorrow afternoon," Elvira replied. "I'll pick you up then."

Hudson was glad that he had another alternative.

"Actually, I'm going to Sir Anthony's *funeral* with Sir Reginald. Why don't I meet you at the *solicitor's* office instead?"

"That's fine by me."

After giving Hudson the *solicitor's* address, Elvira hung up. Hudson sat back in his chair.

Tomorrow is going to be an interesting day, he thought as he *stared* at the photo of the *blackmailer*.

Übung 85: Haben die Wörter dieselbe Bedeutung? Markieren Sie mit richtig ✔ oder falsch – !

1. earlier than/before ☐
2. cease/go ☐
3. vouch/lie ☐
4. impressed/bored ☐
5. ingredient/part ☐
6. solicitor/lawyer ☐
7. maybe/perhaps ☐

Miss Paddington had a nice dinner prepared for Inspector Hudson when he arrived home that evening. Miss Paddington found him looking at a picture of a person wearing a *baggy* jogging suit and a baseball cap.
"Inspector Hudson."
Hudson looked up. "Yes, Miss Paddington."
"Is that picture related to the death of Sir Anthony Baker?"
"It could be. At the moment, I don't know for sure."
"I had lunch today with my friend Hannah. You know, Michael Baker's housekeeper."
"That's right. I remember."
Hudson placed the picture on the side table and gave Miss Paddington his full attention. If she was talking to him about Michael Baker's housekeeper, she must have some news related to the *case*.
"She said that Michael Baker has been really nervous since his father's death. And he's been meeting strange men and receiving strange phone calls."
"What kind of strange men and phone calls?"
"She doesn't know for sure, but she thinks that it may have something to do with his *gambling*," Miss Paddington continued.

"Of course she doesn't want to say bad things about her employer and she's not a *gossip*…"

"But…," Hudson encouraged Miss Paddington to finish her sentence.

"She's worried about him and what he'll do to get money at this point. The reading of the *will* is very important to him."

"Maybe that explains why we've found him going through papers at his father's home and the office. Thank you for the information, Miss Paddington."

"I hope it helps," she replied.

ÜBUNG 86

Übung 86: Verwandeln Sie die Sätze in die direkte Rede!

1. She asked me how I felt.

How do you feel?

2. They told him that Adam was not there.

3. He said that he didn't recognize that woman.

4. She said that they were getting engaged.

5. She said that Michael was worried about money.

6. She said she would call if the blackmailer called again.

Inspector Hudson had problems sleeping when he finally went to bed that night. In his dreams he was *chasing* a figure wearing a huge jogging suit and a baseball cap. He could hear the *blackmailer* repeating words from a children's story: "Run, run as fast as you can. You can't catch me, I'm the Gingerbread Man."
Hudson *tossed and turned* in his bed.
"I will catch you," he heard himself saying in his dream. And then he woke up again.
There was something about the *blackmailer's* voice that seemed *familiar*. What surprised him even more was that he could have sworn that the voice was female, not male. He sat up in his bed and turned the light on. The photo was on his night table. He placed it closer to the light. Normally, when he looked at a photo, he studied the body and tried to see a face under the baseball cap. This time, when he looked at the *blackmailer's* head, he saw something that seemed to *sparkle*. Could that be an earring? he thought. Was that what my *subconscious* had seen that made me hear a woman's voice when the *blackmailer* spoke in my dream? I'll have this picture scanned and *blown up* tomorrow morning. I may be able to uncover something that I've missed so far. I think I'll have a talk with Tony Barrington as well. I should probably *confirm* what Stella Baker told me about Adam Jones's knee. Satisfied with his plan for the next day, Hudson turned off the light and finally fell asleep.

Übung 87: Enträtseln Sie folgende Definitionen!

1. a sound you make when you are in pain or are unhappy:
   ________________ (oamn)

2. to say that something is right or true: ______________ (fomncri)

3. to make something bigger than it was before: ______________ (pu lwbo)

4. to shine in the light: ______________ (prealks)

5. the part of your mind that remembers information you are not trying to remember: ______________ (bsssccnuuooi)

The next morning, Hudson was happy to see Sergeant Brooks at the coffee machine.

"Sergeant," he said to Brooks. "Could you scan this photo for me? I need to see some of the finer details."

Sergeant Brooks looked at the photo. "Yes, I can do that. What exactly are you looking for?"

"Any identifying *features*. Especially anything that would help me identify if we are looking at a man or a woman. "Oh, and this one." Hudson showed Sergeant Brooks the photograph on his mobile phone. "Can you make the woman look younger?"

"Younger, sir?"

"Yes, younger. Can you do it?"

"Yes, sir. Should I do it right now, Inspector?"

"Right after lunch will be fine."

After leaving Sergeant Brooks, Inspector Hudson went to see Tony Barrington in the *forensics* laboratory.

"I see I came at the right time," Hudson said as he watched Barrington return a *corpse* to the freezer. "I was just *curious* about what you were able to find out about Adam Jones."

Barrington took off his gloves and went to wash his hands.

"His death was caused by a *blunt* instrument, just as I thought. Apart from that there's not much I can tell you. One of his knees was in really bad shape. But it had nothing to do with his death."
"Skiing accident," Hudson replied.
"How do you know that?"
"Stella Baker told me. Seems as if it caused him to *limp*."
"It probably did."
"Thanks, Tony."

Übung 88: Fügen Sie die passenden Satzhälften zusammen!

ÜBUNG 88 !

1. ☐ Does any of this
2. ☐ Death was caused by
3. ☐ What exactly
4. ☐ You've been
5. ☐ It would have taken

a) a big help.
b) support any of your theories?
c) a blunt instrument.
d) a long time.
e) are you looking for?

Elvira looked at her watch. There were still ten minutes before the reading of the *will* started. Heavy traffic had kept her from arriving as early as she had planned. She drove around the block several times before finding a place to park her sports car. As she got out of the car, she looked for Inspector Hudson's Bentley. Elvira walked towards the *solicitor's* office. As she *approached* the door, she saw Daphne Edwards and Peter Johnson. They were standing very close to each other. Elvira slowed down, hoping to see more before they saw her. Even so, it did not take long for them to see her.
"Hello, Miss Elliot," Peter Johnson said. "I didn't know you were going to be here today."
"I'm representing the *insurance* company," replied Elvira.

Both *brewery employees* seemed to be happy with her explanation. "After you," Peter Johnson said as he opened the door to the *solicitor's* office.

Elvira greeted the *solicitor* and then took a seat at the back of the room next to Bonnie and Finmore. Stella Baker, Nathan Ramsey, and Michael Baker were sitting in the front *row*. Peter Johnson and Daphne Edwards sat down behind the immediate family. Elvira looked at her watch. It was two o'clock. Where is Hudson? she thought.

The *solicitor* pulled a *manila envelope* out of his desk and started the *proceedings*.

"As you know, you are all here at the request of Sir Anthony."

He opened the envelope with a gold letter opener. After placing the letter opener on the edge of his desk, he took a video out of the envelope.

Michael Baker laughed. "That's typical of father to be melodramatic."

"Michael," Stella *scolded* her brother.

The *solicitor* continued. "Sir Anthony left his last *will* and testament on this video tape. There is also a written and signed version."

With that, Sir Anthony's *solicitor* put the video tape in the player and pressed the start button.

ÜBUNG 89 !

Übung 89: Lesen Sie weiter und unterstreichen Sie die richtige Variante!

Inspector Hudson (1.) watched/looked at his (2.) clock/watch as he (3.) drove/rode his Bentley at (4.) height/high speed. It was ten minutes (5.) after/afterwards two. Several police cars were (6.) on top of/behind him. (7.) All/None of them were on the way to Sir

Anthony's *solicitor's* (8.) office/*plant*. Hudson had called Elvira Elliot to tell her that he had *solved* the *case*, but had been greeted by her voicemail. I hope she is not (9.) at/in danger, he thought.

After the *funeral*, he had met with Sergeant Brooks. Together they had looked at the enlarged photograph of the *blackmailer*. Sir Reginald had recognized the younger face of the woman in the photograph from Peter Johnson's desk. Hudson put his foot on the *accelerator*.

Five minutes later, Inspector Hudson and his colleagues arrived at the office. The policemen got out of their cars and gathered around Hudson, who gave them orders.

"Men, you stay *posted* here. I don't think there will be any *violence*. Still, be prepared for anything. Sergeant Brooks, come with me."

The two men walked towards the building that housed the office of Sir Anthony's *solicitor* and were soon at the office door. Inspector Hudson quietly opened it without knocking. Elvira was the only person who looked at the door as he entered. Everyone was watching the video on the screen. Hudson recognized the man speaking. It was Sir Anthony.

"...and I am selling my company to the holding company owned by Nathan Ramsey."

Stella Baker and Nathan Ramsey *hugged* each other. Sir Anthony continued to speak.

Übung 90: Beantworten Sie die Fragen zum Text!

ÜBUNG 90 !

1. Where does Hudson tell the policemen to stay?

....

2. Who goes into the building with Hudson?

3. Does Hudson think there will be any need to shoot anyone?

4. What is everyone doing when Hudson enters the solicitor's office?

5. Why do Nathan Ramsey and Stella hug each other?

"Shit," Michael said quietly.

Peter stood up quickly. "Damn him. I'm the one who should be running the company."

Sir Anthony's *solicitor* put the tape on pause. "Mr Johnson, please control yourself."

"Peter, don't," Daphne said.

"I should have got the company," Peter Johnson shouted. "I'm…"

"Sir Anthony's *illegitimate* son," Hudson said from the doorway. "Your mother was a popular waitress at Epsom Downs years ago. She and Sir Anthony had an affair. You are their child."

"You?" Stella said, clearly shocked.

Everyone in the room was *staring* at Peter Johnson.

"Yes, me," Peter *sneered*. "Clever of you, Inspector Hudson. What else have you *figured out*?"

"Enough to ask that you and Ms Edwards come with me to the station."

Sergeant Brooks *appeared* behind Inspector Hudson.

Peter looked around like a *caged* animal. Suddenly he ran to the *solicitor's* desk and picked up the letter opener. The *solicitor* stepped back. Peter Johnson *grabbed* Stella Baker and pointed the letter opener at her throat. Bonnie screamed. Finmore pulled her close to him. Michael Baker opened his mouth, but words did not come out. He looked *confused*. Nathan Ramsey moved towards Stella and Peter Johnson.

"If anyone comes near me, she's dead!" Peter Johnson *yelled*.

"Peter!" Daphne screamed. "Not another death. She's your half-sister."

"I tried to stop him from killing Adam, Inspector," Daphne said quickly. "I really did. Adam just made him so angry. He *threatened* to tell Stella that we were using the blackmail money to buy the company."

"The fool! After six months he suddenly developed a *conscience*. I think he was in love with you, dear sister," Peter *hissed* at Stella, *sneering*.

He started to move towards the door, keeping Stella close to his body and the letter opener at her throat. "Move aside, Inspector. You too, Officer."

Hudson followed Peter's directions. So did Sergeant Brooks. Peter laughed again, hysterically, and exited the room with Stella.

"Now close the door."

Hudson closed the door.

Übung 91: Lesen Sie weiter und unterstreichen Sie die richtige Variante!

"What are you (1.) making/doing?" Nathan Ramsey screamed. "He's (2.) getting/going away with Stella."

"He won't get (3.) long/far," Hudson said *forcefully*. He had already pulled (4.) out/off his gun and opened the door.
At that moment they heard a scream (5.) inside/outside.
"Stella!" Nathan Ramsey ran (6.) towards/through the door. Sergeant Brooks stopped him. Outside, Stella was on the ground. Inspector Hudson ran over to her.

"I'm all right. He went that way," she said, pointing to the exit. Inspector Hudson ran towards the door and saw Peter Johnson running across the street. Hudson signalled for the officers to stop him. Peter ran towards the right, but stopped when he saw several officers running towards him. He then turned and ran to the left, but more officers were blocking his way. A police car drove up, keeping him from crossing the street again. Inspector Hudson smiled. Peter Johnson was *trapped*.

Half an hour after Peter Johnson and Daphne Edwards had been taken away, everyone had *calmed down* again. They decided to stay and listen to the rest of Sir Anthony's *will* and testament. Finmore and Bonnie were extremely surprised to receive his life *insurance* money and very happy to find out that they could finally *retire*. When it was over, Stella Baker *approached* Hudson and Elvira.
"I don't know how I'll ever be able to thank you," she said.
Hudson *assured her* that the words she had just spoken were enough.

ÜBUNG 92 !

Übung 92: Vervollständigen Sie die Wendungen mit ***do*** *oder* ***make****!*

1. ____________ a move

2. ____________ nothing at all

3. __________ someone a favour

4. __________ someone angry

5. __________ your work

6. __________ a fortune

As they left the building, Elvira *quizzed* Hudson. "How did you know that Peter Johnson was Sir Anthony's *illegitimate* son and the trio were *blackmailing* Stella Baker?"
"Sergeant Brooks *blew up* the picture of the person who picked up the money. Upon closer inspection it was easy to see that it was a woman with dark hair, wearing very *baggy* clothes. So I *assumed* it could be Daphne Edwards. And then I knew that Peter Johnson reminded me of someone. You remember that picture I found in Peter Johnson's desk? It was a picture of him and his mother. Sergeant Brooks made the woman look younger, and Sir Reginald recognized her. He remembered that she had worked at the Epsom Downs. All of the *evidence* was *circumstantial*, but Peter Johnson didn't know that."
Inspector Hudson's mobile phone rang. He recognized Sir Reginald's number.

Übung 93: Lesen Sie weiter und setzen Sie das richtige Wort ein!
(better, company, heart pills, illegitimate, mother, truth, working)

ÜBUNG 93 !

"James! Glad I caught you. Good job. Peter Johnson and Daphne Edwards have just *confessed* to everything. Johnson went to see Anthony on Saturday to talk about the (1.) __________________.

Or that's what he told Anthony. In reality he planned to tell him that he was his (2.) ______________ son. He had found this out upon the death of his (3.) ______________. He had been (4.) ______________ at the company for years, slowly *gaining Anthony's trust*. *Apparently*, Anthony even told him that he would have made a (5.) ______________ son than Michael. But when Johnson told him the (6.) ______________, Anthony was so shocked he started to have *chest* pains. We know the rest. He *intentionally* didn't give Anthony his (7.) ______________."

Hudson heard Sir Reginald *sigh*, before the Chief Inspector continued. "And regarding the blackmailing, he decided to *blackmail* Stella one night when Daphne Edwards and Adam Jones were joking about buying the company. Peter Johnson saw his chance, but he didn't have enough money. He told Daphne Edwards and Adam Jones about his background. The three of them decided to *blackmail* Stella. When Adam wanted to stop, the two men fought and Peter Johnson killed Adam. Daphne Edwards thought that he had *got rid of* Adam's body. That's why she *fainted* when she found out the body was still in the *plant*. They *blackmailed* Stella because they knew she would pay to protect the family name. Michael would have laughed in their faces. What did he *inherit*, by the way?"

"The house," Hudson said.

"That should keep him happy. Anyway, *treat* yourself and that nice Miss Elliot *to* a good dinner tonight."

Hudson smiled. "I will, sir. I will."

Übung 94: Personenbezeichnungen. Wie heißen die Personen, die die angegebenen Tätigkeiten ausführen?

ÜBUNG 94

1. drive — *driver*
2. investigate — ______
3. keep house — ______
4. gamble — ______
5. blackmail — ______
6. design — ______

Abschlusstest

Übung 1: Fügen Sie den gesuchten Begriff ein!

1. there's ________________ than meets the eye

2. keep an ________________ on someone

3. count your ________________ before they're hatched

4. the ________________ on the cake

5. as ________________ as thieves

6. kick the ________________

7. drag a good name through the ________________

Übung 2: Welche Bedeutung haben die folgenden Sätze? Kreuzen Sie die passende Erklärung an!

1. Miss Elliot seemed to be very impressed by Peter Johnson.
a) ☐ She thought he was very clever and good-looking.
b) ☐ She found it very stressful listening to him.

2. He was very reluctant to go with her.
a) ☐ He couldn't wait to go with her.
b) ☐ He wasn't at all happy about going with her.

3. He's the CFO of the company.
a) ☐ He is the Chief Financial Officer.
b) ☐ He is the Chef Financial Officer.

4. Peter bumped into Inspector Hudson.
a) ☐ Peter's car hit Inspector Hudson's car.
b) ☐ Peter walked into Inspector Hudson with force.

5. Sir Anthony's arm was numb.
a) ☐ His arm was broken.
b) ☐ He had no feeling in his arm.

6. They were double-crossing Adam.
a) ☐ They were lying to Adam by working on their own plan.
b) ☐ They didn't know where Adam was.

Übung 3: Welche Synonyme gehören zusammen? Ordnen Sie zu!

1. ☐ corpse	a) stop
2. ☐ provide	b) shout
3. ☐ cease	c) be useful
4. ☐ muse	d) dead body
5. ☐ confirm	e) give
6. ☐ yell	f) think
7. ☐ be convenient	g) agree

Übung 4: Wie heißt das Simple Past und Past Participle der folgenden Verben?

1. see ______________ ______________

2. catch ______________ ______________

3. wake ______________ ______________

4. meet ______ ______

5. know ______ ______

6. hide ______ ______

7. understand ______ ______

Übung 5: Unterstreichen Sie die richtige Variante!

1. Hudson tossed and tipped/turned all night.
2. I'm looking for a manila/vanilla envelope.
3. Adam was killed by a numb/blunt instrument.
4. Nathan Ramsey stayed under/over last night.
5. He was custom/accustomed to something different.
6. Stella is with her finance/fiancé.
7. The barrels were neatly stocked/stacked on top of each other.

Übung 6: Übersetzen Sie die Begriffe ins Englische!

1. erben ______

2. Geschwister ______

3. verdächtig ______

4. die Themse ______

5. in Ohnmacht fallen ______

6. einen Blick werfen ______

7. Erpressung ______

Übung 7: Welche Gegenteile gehören zusammen?

1. ☐ mansion	a) by chance
2. ☐ forcefully	b) sharp
3. ☐ employer	c) thief
4. ☐ secret	d) faintly
5. ☐ solicitor	e) employee
6. ☐ blunt	f) public
7. ☐ on purpose	g) criminal
8. ☐ inspector	h) tent

Übung 8: Setzen Sie die richtige Form des Verbs ein!

1. They (fight) ________________ when the two investigators entered the room.
2. I (not think) ________________ that Adam is in the building.
3. We (found) ________________ the blackmailer.
4. Michael (stop) ____________ arguing with his father when he saw that people were listening to them.
5. I (design) ______________________ dresses since I received my inheritance.
6. Elvira (wait) ___________ for two hours and then left.
7. Stella (not tell) ___________ Hudson about her boyfriend.

Übung 9: Setzen Sie den richtigen Artikel bzw. die richtige Präposition ein!

1. I want to see you here ________ my London club immediately.
2. They had ________ big fight.
3. He had not received any ________ this information from Sir Reginald.
4. What is all of this ________?
5. He's ________ officer.
6. She was the subject ________ their conversation.
7. Give me ________ call if you think of anything else.

Übung 10: Antworten Sie auf Englisch!

1. Who is Stella Baker's half-brother?

____

2. Who is the new owner of the brewery?

____

3. What does Michael Baker inherit?

____

4. Where did Sir Anthony's killer first reveal himself?

____

5. Why did Sir Anthony have a heart attack?

____

Lösungen

Übung 1: 1. gefühllos 2. verbessern 3. leiden 4. das Gesicht verziehen 5. vorbeiflitzen 6. Erleichterung 7. Ernährung 8. Brust(korb)
Übung 2: 1. Inspector Hudson was reading the paper happily. 2. Hudson looked quickly at the front page. 3. Hudson listened patiently to Sir Reginald. 4. He rose slowly. 5. The sun was shining brightly. 6. Hudson sat comfortably in his chair.
Übung 3: 1. large house/mansion 2. crying/sobbing 3. policeman/constable 4. not normal/strange 5. dead body/corpse 6. asked/inquired
Übung 4: 1. body 2. housekeeper 3. active 4. pointed 5. glasses 6. over
Übung 5: 1. estimated 2. evidence 3. slumped 4. staff 5. stared
Übung 6: 1. Bonnie is a **plump** woman. 2. Bonnie and Finmore are **married**. 3. She **sniffed** as she spoke to Inspector Hudson. 4. I think there is more than meets the **eye** here. 5. Tony Barrington is a forensics **genius**. 6. Finmore **shrugged** in response to the question.
Übung 7: 1. d 2. e 3. f 4. b 5. a 6. c
Übung 8: 1. questioning 2. mention 3. subject 4. mind 5. chair 6. arthritis 7. mansion
Übung 9: 1. tell 2. knew 3. losing 4. wanted 5. didn't have 6. has
Ubung 10: 1. falsch 2. richtig 3. falsch 4. falsch 5. richtig 6. falsch 7. falsch
Übung 11: 1. fight 2. closest 3. hole 4. myself 5. heard 6. state 7. golf 8. surely
Übung 12: 1. Sir Anthony fought with his son, Michael. 2. Inspector Hudson was leaning against the bar of the golf club. 3. He left the golf club around four o'clock. 4. He decided to listen to the conversation between Arthur and John. 5. He had met the club manager once before when Hudson had come to see Sir Reginald at the club. 6. The four men went to the club manager's office to talk.
Übung 13: 1. Please bear with me until I have questioned everyone. 2. He cocked his head to one side. 3. If my memory serves me right, you are Inspector Hudson. 4. I don't want people to jump to the wrong conclusion. 5. There's more to this case than meets the eye. 6. His life flashed by.
Übunt 14: 1. might 2. alive 3. Inspector 4. likely 5. club 6. someone 7. waiting
Übung 15: 1. He said I didn't have the right to make decisions about the family fortune. 2. He said if he wanted my opinion, he would ask for it. 3. He

asked what I was doing at the Epsom Golf Club. 4. He said he hadn't even started to embarrass me. 5. He said he wanted me there at his London club. 6. He said I didn't have the right to talk to him like that. 7. He said he had seen him leave the club.

Übung 16: 1. d 2. e 3. f 4. a 5. b 6. c

Übung 17: 1. at 2. in 3. at 4. back 5. of 6. for 7. in 8. out

Übung 18: 1. respectable 2. hug 3. know 4. enemy 5. poor 6. give 7. victim

Übung 19: 1. f 2. e 3. g 4. a 5. c 6. h 7. d 8. b

Übung 20: 1. c 2. g 3. e 4. f 5. a 6. b 7. d

Übung 21: 1. meant 2. prepare 3. echoed 4. pay 5. bear with me 6. love 7. put 8. was waiting

Übung 22: 1. delay 2. expect 3. it is 4. proper 5. coat 6. late 7. figures

Übung 23: 3, 5, 1, 4, 2, 6

Übung 24: 1. Rumour has it that Michael expects to inherit the fortune. 2. Count me in! 3. He did not die from natural causes. 4. The same thought crossed my mind. 5. He wants to cash in. 6. I think his death was caused by foul play. 7. Michael never lived up to his father's expectations.

Übung 25: 1. completely 2. about 3. sitting 4. looking 5. for 6. think 7. in

Übung 26: 1. c 2. e 3. b 4. f 5. a 6. g 7. d

Übung 27: 1. g 2. c 3. f 4. e 5. b 6. a 7. d

Übung 28: 1. will 2. is going to 3. is going to 4. will 5. will 6. are going to 7. will

Übung 29: 1. c 2. e 3. b 4. f 5. a 6. g 7. d

Übung 30: 1. towards 2. at 3. in 4. at 5. of 6. about 7. for 8. by

Übung 31: 1. murder 2. brewery 3. bill 4. enemies 5. crying 6. natural causes 7. divorce

Übung 32: 1. falsch 2. falsch 3. richtig 4. richtig 5. richtig 6. falsch 7. falsch 8. richtig

Übung 33: 1. b 2. a 3. b 4. a 5. b 6. a 7. b

Übung 34: 1. something 2. policy 3. in 4. related 5. hold 6. match 7. necessary 8. In spite of 9. start

Übung 35: 1. They had scones with clotted cream. 2. Michael Baker made money gambling. 3. Stella is a dress designer. 4. Sir Reginald is a close family friend. 5. There are two damp glasses with no fingerprints at the crime scene and there are no prints on the bottle of pills. 6. She is very protective of Stella.

Übung 36: 1. fortune 2. confident 3. apron 4. silent 5. attacked 6. refused

Übung 37: 1. approach 2. off duty 3. silk 4. gamble 5. neat 6. prim
Übung 38: 1. Sie ist neidisch auf ihren Bruder. 2. Er erbte Geld von seinem Vater. 3. Sir Anthony will, dass die Brauerei erhalten wird. 4. Michael Baker soll den Tag nicht vor dem Abend loben. 5. Sie hat einen verschwenderischen Lebenswandel. 6. Er hat keinen Geschäftssinn.
Übung 39: "Finally!" Elvira exclaimed twenty minutes later as she brought the car to a halt. "I thought I was going to fall asleep behind the wheel."
Inspector Hudson laughed to himself. He knew that it must have been hard for Elvira to drive so slowly.
She and Stella Baker may share the same taste in dresses, but Stella definitely wasn't a fan of high speed, Hudson thought.
Übung 40: 1. c 2. f 3. d 4. b 5. a 6. e
Übung 41: 1. at 2. in 3. on, of 4. for 5. to
Übung 42: 1. e 2. d 3. a 4. g 5. f 6. c 7. b
Übung 43: 1. several 2. bring 3. illegitimate 4. last 5. rival 6. temper 7. world
Übung 44: 1. house 2. prim 3. interest 4. puzzled 5. pocket 6. picture 7. meeting
Übung 45: 1. Hudson thinks that there are four possible suspects. 2. Elvira may have more information by Monday afternoon. 3. The photograph may help him find the blackmailer. 4. She was worried about Stella. 5. The four suspects are Michael, Stella, their half-brother, and the blackmailer. 6. She does not have the blackmailer's phone number. It appears as unlisted. 7. Stella Baker's housekeeper took the picture.
Übung 46: 1. falsch 2. richtig 3. falsch 4. richtig 5. richtig 6. falsch
Übung 47: 1. Everything changed when John died. 2. His sister said that he gambles. 3. It was taken care of off the record. 4. He turned a blind eye while John was alive. 5. Don't drag our good name through the mud. 6. He has got into lots of trouble lately.
Übung 48: 1. d 2. g 3. c 4. a 5. f 6. e 7. b
Übung 49: 1. for 2. to 3. in 4. about 5. of
Übung 50: 1. sale 2. company 3. owned 4. heard of 5. businessman 6. high
Übung 51: 1. since 2. for 3. ago 4. ago 5. for 6. for 7. for 8. since
Übung 52: 1. a 2. b 3. b 4. a 5. a 6. b 7. b
Übung 53: 1. f 2. g 3. a 4. b 5. c 6. e 7. d
Übung 54: 3, 1, 2, 4
Übung 55: 1. Michael is going to throw out the staff if he inherits the brewery. 2. Nathan Ramsey is going out with Stella. 3. Michael had shown how irresponsible he was once again. 4. Many of the breweries are consoli-

dating. 5. Sir Anthony's company produces beer. 6. Bonnie and Finmore are the beneficiaries of Sir Anthony's insurance policy.

Übung 56: 1. Can I help you? 2. We would like to ask you a few questions. 3. I have not done anything illegal. 4. Can we go into your office to talk? 5. I do not have much choice. 6. This is my colleague, Miss Elliot.

Übung 57: 1. c 2. a 3. e 4. f 5. b 6. d

Übung 58: 1. a whole load of 2. lose one's temper 3. offer your condolences 4. kick the bucket 5. sympathetically 6. get on 7. reluctant

Übung 59: 1. another 2. are 3. sell 4. that 5. last 6. there 7. week's

Übung 60: 1. Someone has been in this room. 2. Hudson has searched for many criminals. 3. The blackmailer has called back. 4. Stella's housekeeper has seen the blackmailer. 5. Hudson has found the murderer. 6. Michael has shut the door.

Übung 61: 1. falsch 2. falsch 3. falsch 4. richtig 5. falsch 6. richtig

Übung 62: 1. b 2. a 3. b 4. b 5. a

Übung 63: 1. wives 2. inquiries 3. companies 4. breweries 5. wishes 6. people 7. businesses 8. information

Übung 64: 1. hour (our) 2. informations (information) 3. Patients (Patents) 4. throan (thrown) 5. want (what) 6. laufing (laughing) 7. aded (added) 8. onion (opinion)

Übung 65: 1. did 2. made 3. doing 4. do 5. made 6. make 7. make

Übung 66: 1. business cards 2. hall 3. door 4. either 5. likely 6. group 7. seemed

Übung 67: 1. a 2. b 3. a 4. b 5. b

Übung 68: 1. too 2. to 3. to, to 4. too, to 5. too

Übung 69: 1. an 2. – 3. – 4. a 5. – 6. an 7. a

Übung 70: 1. as thick as thieves 2. give it a go 3. kick the bucket 4. live life in the fast lane 5. turn a blind eye 6. go down the drain 7. offer him my condolences

Übung 71: 1. muttered 2. finished 3. remain 4. until 5. said 6. think 7. death 8. company

Übung 72: 1. c 2. d 3. h 4. g 5. b 6. e 7. a 8. f

Übung 73: 1. on site 2. double-cross 3. keep an eye on 4. back us 5. board of directors 6. highest bidder 7. down payment

Übung 74: 1. for 2. right 3. worry 4. anywhere 5. remember 6. left 7. anything 8. by

Übung 75: 1. out 2. at 3. to 4 up 5. about 6. up 7. off

Übung 76: 1. blunt 2. disturbing 3. stacked 4. motive 5. voluntarily 6. brewery 7. figure
Übung 77: 1. some 2. some 3. any 4. any 5. some 6. some 7. any
Übung 78: 1. told 2. made 3. died 4. took 5. inherited 6. had been 7. left 8. sat
Übung 79: 1. a 2. b 3. b 4. a 5. a 6. b 7. a
Übung 80: 1. serious 2. compose 3. spread 4. squeezed 5. accustomed 6. puzzled 7. blackmailer
Übung 81: 1. She needs to talk to him about the funeral. 2. They want to find out if she had anything to do with Adam's death. 3. He was found wearing a baggy jogging suit and he had an envelope in his pocket. 4. The will states who the new owner of the company will be. 5. It was found in the plant. 6. She fainted. 7. Her emotions are mixed.
Übung 82: 1. forcefully 2. an 3. delivering 4. been 5. why 6. picked 7. can
Übung 83: 1. Who 2. Whose 3. When 4. Where 5. Why 6. How 7. What
Übung 84: 1. Adam was in the plant. 2. Sir Reginald knows the identity of the woman in the picture. 3. Everyone knew that Stella was being blackmailed. 4. Elvira likes Inspector Hudson's Bentley. 5. Sir Anthony found his pills. 6. Michael Baker was very clever. 7. Michael has been told about his half-brother.
Übung 85: 1. richtig 2. falsch 3. falsch 4. falsch 5. richtig 6. richtig 7. richtig
Übung 86: 1. How do you feel? 2. Adam is not here. 3. I don't recognize that woman. 4. We are getting engaged. 5. Michael is worried about money. 6. I will call if the blackmailer calls again.
Übung 87: 1. moan 2. confirm 3. blow up 4. sparkle 5. subconscious
Übung 88: 1. b 2. c 3. e 4. a 5. d
Übung 89: 1. looked 2. watch 3. drove 4. high 5. after 6. behind 7. All 8. office 9. in
Übung 90: 1. Hudson tells them to stay posted outside the building. 2. Sergeant Brooks goes into the building with Hudson. 3. No, he does not think there will be any violence. 4. They are watching the video made by Sir Anthony. 5. Sir Anthony has agreed to sell the brewery to Nathan Ramsey.
Übung 91: 1. doing 2. getting 3. far 4. out 5. outside 6. towards
Übung 92: 1. make 2. do 3. do 4. make 5. do 6. make
Übung 93: 1. company 2. illegitimate 3. mother 4. working 5. better 6. truth 7. heart pills
Übung 94: 1. driver 2. investigator 3. housekeeper 4. gambler 5. blackmailer 6. designer

Lösungen Abschlusstest

Übung 1: more 2. eye 3. chickens 4. icing 5. thick 6. bucket 7. mud
Übung 2: 1. a 2. b 3. a 4. b 5. b 6. a
Übung 3: 1. d 2. e 3. a 4. f 5. g 6. b 7. c
Übung 4: 1. saw/seen 2. caught/caught 3. woke/woken 4. met/met 5. knew/known 6. hid/hidden 6. understood/understood
Übung 5: 1. turned 2. manila 3. blunt 4. over 5. accustomed 6. fiancé 7. stacked
Übung 6: 1. inherit 2. siblings 3. suspicious 4. the Thames 5. faint 6. glance at 7. blackmail
Übung 7: 1. h 2. d 3. e 4. f 5. g 6. b 7. a 8. c
Übung 8: 1. were fighting 2. don't think 3. have found 4. stopped 5. have been designing 6. waited 7. didn't tell
Übung 9: 1. at 2. a 3. of 4. about 5. an 6. of 7. a
Übung 10: 1. Peter Johnson is Stella Baker's half-brother. 2. Nathan Ramsey's holding company is the new owner of the brewery. 3. Michael Baker inherits the house. 4. He first revealed himself at the reading of the will. 5. Sir Anthony was so shocked when Peter Johnson told him that he was his son that he had a heart attack.

Glossar

fam	umgangssprachlich
fig	bildlich
pl	Plural
v	Verb

accompany *v*	begleiten
accuse *v* **sb. (of sth.)**	jmd. (einer Sache) beschuldigen
according to sb.	jmd. zufolge, laut jmd.
aches and pains *fam*	Wehwehchen *fam*, Schmerzen
admit *v*	zugeben
affairs *pl*	Angelegenheiten
afford *v* **sth.**	sich etw. leisten
announce *v*	bekanntgeben, verkünden
anxious	bestrebt, ungeduldig; besorgt
apparently	anscheinend, offensichtlich
appear *v*	(er)scheinen, auftauchen
approach *v*	sich nähern
approve *v* **(of) sth.**	billigen, gutheißen; genehmigen
apron	Schürze
asking price	geforderter Preis, Angebotspreis
assume *v*	annehmen
assure *v* **sb.**	jmd. versichern, (dass) …
as thick as thieves	wie Pech und Schwefel zusammenhalten
astonish *v*	erstaunen
auditor	Rechnungsprüfer(in)
avoid *v*	vermeiden
awkward	unbehaglich, unangenehm, peinlich
back *v* **sb.**	jmd. unterstützen
badge	Dienstmarke
baggy	weit, schlabberig
barely	kaum
barrel	Fass

be *v* **accustomed to (doing) sth.**	etw. gewohnt sein, gewohnt sein, etw. zu tun
bear *v* **with sb.**	mit jmd. Geduld haben
be *v* **awarded sth.**	etw. zugesprochen bekommen, erhalten
be *v* **deep in thought**	(ganz) in Gedanken versunken sein
behaviour	Benehmen
behind-the-scenes	hinter den Kulissen agierend
be *v* **in charge**	zuständig sein, die Verantwortung tragen
beneficiary	Begünstigte(r)
benefit *v* **sb.**	jmd. nützen
bet (bet, bet) *v*	wetten
blackmail *v*	erpressen
blackmailer	Erpresser(in)
blink *v*	blinzeln
blow	Stoß, Schlag
blow (blew, blown) *v* **sth. up**	*hier:* etw. vergrößern; etw. aufblasen
blunt	stumpf
blush *v*	erröten
board of directors	Vorstand, Aufsichtrat
borough	Stadtbezirk
bother *v* **sb.**	jmd. belästigen, jmd. stören
brake *v*	bremsen
brewery	Bierbrauerei
bring *v* **sb. to justice**	jmd. vor Gericht bringen
bulk	Großteil
bump *v* **against**	zusammenstoßen mit
bump *v* **into sb.** *fam*	jmd. zufällig in die Arme laufen
buyout	Aufkauf
caged	gefangen, eingesperrt
calm *v* **(sb.) down**	(jmd./sich) beruhigen
case	Fall, Sache
cash *v* **in**	zu Geld machen, einlösen
cease *v*	aufhören

CEO (Chief Executive Officer)	Geschäftsführer(in)
change *v* **one's mind**	es sich anders überlegen, die Meinung ändern
chat *v*	sich unterhalten
check *v* **(on) sth.**	etw. überprüfen
cheerful	fröhlich
chest	Brust(korb)
choice	Wahl
choke *v* **on sth.**	sich an etw. verschlucken
circumstances *pl*	Umstände
circumstantial evidence	Indizienbeweis
claim *v*	behaupten; in Anspruch nehmen
clear *v* **one's throat**	sich räuspern
clotted cream	stichfester Rahm mit hohem Fettanteil
cock *v* **one's head**	den Kopf auf die Seite legen
come *v* **in handy**	gelegen kommen
comfort *v*	trösten
competitive	konkurrenzfähig
compose *v* **oneself**	sich beruhigen, sich zusammen nehmen
conclude *v*	folgern, beschließen
conduct *v* **sth.**	etw. (durch)führen
confess *v*	gestehen, beichten
confidently	selbstbewusst; zuversichtlich
confirm *v*	bestätigen
confused	verwirrt
conscience	Gewissen
consolidate *v*	sich zusammenschließen
constable	Polizist(in)
contribute *v*	beitragen
convenient	praktisch
convertible	Cabrio
convince *v*	überzeugen

corporate head office	Konzernzentrale
corpse	Leiche
Count me in! *fam*	Ich bin dabei!
count one's chickens before they're hatched *fig*	den Tag vor dem Abend loben *fig*
cover *v* **sth. up**	etw. vertuschen
crime scene	Tatort
crookedly	schief, krumm
cross *v* **one's mind**	jmd. durch den Kopf gehen, einfallen
curb	Bordstein
curious(ly)	neugierig
curse	Fluch
damp	feucht
delicious	köstlich
deliver *v*	(aus)liefern
delivery	Lieferung
demanding	fordernd, anspruchsvoll
detect *v*	erkennen, entdecken, wahrnehmen
die *v* **of natural causes**	eines natürlichen Todes sterben
diet	Ernährung, Nahrung; Diät
disappointment	Enttäuschung
discreet(ly)	diskret, taktvoll
disguise *v*	*hier*: verstellen (Stimme); (sich) verkleiden
disgust	Abscheu
distinctive	charakteristisch, ausgeprägt
disturbing	beunruhigend
do *v* **research**	forschen, untersuchen
do *v* **sb. a favour**	jmd. einen Gefallen tun
double-cross *v*	jmd. hintergehen, betrügen
doubt	Zweifel
down payment	Anzahlung
drag *v* **sb./sth. through the mud** *fig*	jmd./etw. durch den Dreck ziehen *fig*

drawer	Schublade
dreadful	fürchterlich
echo *v*	(wider)hallen, nachhallen
effort	Versuch, Anstrengung
embarrassed	verlegen, peinlich berührt
embarrass *v* **sb.**	jmd. in Verlegenheit bringen
employee	Angestellte(r)
employee buyout	Aufkauf durch die Belegschaft
engaged	verlobt
erase *v*	entfernen, löschen
estimated	geschätzt
evidence	Beweis
exaggerate *v*	übertreiben
examine *v* **sth.**	etw. untersuchen
exclaim *v*	ausrufen
expectation	Erwartung
experience *v*	erleben, erfahren
faint *v*	in Ohnmacht fallen
faint(ly)	schwach, kraftlos
familiar	vertraut, bekannt
fasten *v* **sth.**	etw. anlegen, schließen
feature	Merkmal, Besonderheit
fellow *fam*	Kerl, Bursche *fam*
fiancé	Verlobter
figure	*hier:* Zahl, Ziffer; Figur
figure *v* **sth. out** *fig*	etw. herausfinden
fill *v* **sb. in (on sth.)**	jmd. (über etw.) informieren
fingerprint	Fingerabdruck
first-hand	aus erster Hand
fist fight	Faustkampf
fit of rage	Wutanfall
flash *v* **by**	vorbeiflitzen
forceful(ly)	*hier:* entschieden; kraftvoll
forehead	Stirn
forensics	Gerichtsmedizin, Kriminalistik

fortune	*hier:* Vermögen; Schicksal, Glück
foul play	*hier:* Verbrechen (als Todesursache); Foulspiel
frame *v* **sb.** *fig*	jmd. etw. anhängen, jmd. reinlegen
frown *v*	die Stirn runzeln
funeral	Beerdigung
gain *v* **sb.'s trust**	jds. Vertrauen gewinnen
gambling	Glücksspiel, Spielen
gaze	starrer Blick
get *v* **along with sb.**	sich mit jmd. gut verstehen
get *v* **away with sth.**	ungestraft davonkommen
get *v* **rid of sb./sth.**	jmd./etw. loswerden
give *v* **sth. a go**	etw. (aus)probieren
glance *v*	einen Blick werfen, schauen
go *v* **down the drain** *fig*	den Bach runtergehen *fig*, vor die Hunde gehen *fig*
Good heavens!	Großer Gott!, Du lieber Himmel!
good looks	gutes Aussehen
gossip	Klatsch, Tratsch
gossip *v*	klatschen, tratschen
grab *v*	packen, fassen
green	*hier:* Grün, Rasen (Golf)
grimace *v*	das Gesicht verziehen
grunt *v*	ächzen, grunzen
handle *v* **sth.**	etw. handhaben, für etw. zuständig sein
hard-earned	schwer verdient
haughtily	hochmütig, überheblich
have *v* **a fight**	*hier:* Streit haben; kämpfen
head *v*	leiten, führen
headline	Schlagzeile
heart failure	Herzversagen
heir	Erbe/Erbin
heritage	Erbschaft, Erbe
hesitate *v*	zögern

highest bidder	Höchstbietende(r)
hint *v*	andeuten
hiss *v*	fauchen, zischen
Hold tight! *fam*	Festhalten!
hug *v* **sb.**	jmd. umarmen
hunch	Ahnung, Intuition
ID (identification)	Ausweis
I'd (I would) rather…	Ich würde lieber …
icing on the cake *fig*	das Sahnehäubchen *fig*
if my memory serves me right	wenn ich mich recht erinnere
illegitimate	unehelich; unrechtmäßig
imagine *v*	sich vorstellen
impatient(ly)	ungeduldig
imply *v*	andeuten, implizieren
impressed	beeindruckt
improve *v*	verbessern
ingredient	Bestandteil; Zutat
inherit *v*	etw. erben
inheritance	Erbe
innocent(ly)	unschuldig, arglos
inquire *v*	fragen (nach), sich erkundigen
in sb.'s favour	zu jds. Gunsten
insider trading	Insiderhandel (Börse)
insurance	Versicherung
insurance claim	Versicherungsanspruch
insurance policy	Versicherungspolice
insurance premium	Versicherungsprämie
intentionally	absichtlich, vorsätzlich
interfere *v* **with**	etw. beeinträchtigen, stören
interrogate *v* **sb.**	jmd. verhören
in unison	einstimmig, gleichzeitig
investigate *v*	untersuchen, ermitteln
investigation	Untersuchung, Ermittlung
irreplaceable	unersetzlich

irresponsible	unverantwortlich
irritably	gereizt
irritation	Verärgerung
jealousy	Neid; Eifersucht
jump *v*	*hier:* zusammenzucken; springen
jump *v* **to a conclusion** *fig*	voreilige Schlüsse ziehen
justice	Gerechtigkeit
keep *v* **an eye on** *fig*	im Auge behalten
kick *v* **the bucket** *fam*	ins Gras beißen *fam*
kid *v* **oneself** *fam*	sich etw. vormachen
lap	Schoß
lavish	verschwenderisch, großzügig
leaf *v* **through**	durchblättern
lift *v* **sb.'s spirits** *fig*	jds. Stimmung heben
limp	Hinken
limp *v*	hinken
line	*hier:* (Telefon-)Leitung, Linie
line of business	Branche
liquid	flüssig
literally	buchstäblich, im wahrsten Sinne des Wortes
live *v* **life in the fast lane** *fig*	ein Leben auf der Überholspur führen *fig*
live *v* **life to the full**	das Leben in vollen Zügen genießen
live *v* **up to sth.**	etw. erfüllen, etw. gerecht werden
loosen *v* **up**	auflockern
lorry	LKW
lose *v* **one's temper**	die Geduld verlieren, ausrasten
make *v* **a habit of doing sth.**	die Gewohnheit haben, etw. zu tun
manila envelope	brauner Briefumschlag
manners *pl*	Manieren
mansion	Villa, Herrenhaus
march *v*	marschieren
mark my words	lass dir das gesagt sein

member	Mitglied
mention *v*	erwähnen
moan *v*	stöhnen
motion *v*	jmd. ein Zeichen geben, bedeuten
mumble *v*	murmeln, grummeln
muse *v*	grübeln
neatly	ordentlich
no matter what/who …	ganz gleich was/wer …
not give *v* **a damn about sth.** *fam*	sich einen Dreck um etw. scheren *fam*
numb	taub, gefühllos
observe *v*	bemerken, feststellen
obstruction of justice	Strafvereitelung, Behinderung der Justiz
obvious(ly)	offensichtlich
off duty	außer Dienst, dienstfrei
offer *v* **sb. one's condolences**	jmd. sein Beleid aussprechen
offspring	Nachkommen, Nachwuchs
off the record *fam*	inoffiziell, vertraulich
Okay, you've made your point! *fam*	Okay, ich hab's verstanden! *fam*
old-fashioned	altmodisch
on behalf of	im Namen von
oncoming	entgegenkommend, nahend
on purpose	absichtlich, mutwillig
on site	vor Ort
open-and-shut case *fig*	klarer Fall
opportunity	Gelegenheit, Chance
partially	teilweise
particular	besondere(r, s), bestimmt
party	*hier:* Gruppe, Partei; Feier
pat *v*	leicht klopfen, tätscheln
patience	Geduld
patient(ly)	geduldig
pay *v* **sb. a visit**	jmd. einen Besuch abstatten

plant	*hier:* Fertigungsanlage, Fabrik; Pflanze
plump	mollig, rundlich
posted	*hier:* postiert, auf Posten; verschickt
pour *v*	einschenken, gießen
premeditated	vorsätzlich, geplant
premises	Betriebsgelände
presume *v*	annehmen, vermuten
pretend *v*	tun als ob, vorgeben
prevent *v* **sth.**	etw. verhindern
prim	spröde, steif
proceedings	Prozedere, Verfahren
proper(ly)	angemessen, ordentlich
propose *v*	einen Heiratsantrag machen
protective	fürsorglich, beschützend
proudly	stolz
provide *v* **sth.**	etw. zur Verfügung stellen, liefern
purpose	Zweck
puzzled	irritiert, verblüfft
quiz *v* **sb.**	jmd. ausfragen
quote *v*	zitieren
raise *v* **questions**	Fragen aufwerfen
raise *v* **sb.**	jmd. erziehen
raise *v* **sth.**	etw. (an)heben
rattle *v*	scheppern, klappern
reach *v*	greifen, (er)reichen
reach *v* **an agreement**	eine Vereinbarung treffen
refuse *v*	ablehnen, verweigern
relief	Erleichterung
reluctant(ly)	widerwillig, widerstrebend
replacement	Ersatz
representative	Beauftragte(r), Vertreter(in)
reputation	Ruf, Ansehen
resent *v* **sth.**	etw. hassen, sich sehr ärgern über
residence	Anwesen, Wohnsitz

retire *v*	in Ruhestand gehen
retirement	Ruhestand
reveal *v*	enthüllen, aufdecken, zeigen
row	Reihe
rumour has it… *fig*	man munkelt, dass …, Gerüchten zufolge
scold *v*	schimpfen
scone	süßes Hefegebäck (oft mit Rosinen)
secretive	verschlossen, heimlichtuerisch *fam*
serenade *v* **sb.**	jmd. ein Ständchen singen
serious	ernst, ernsthaft
settle *v* **sth.**	etw. regeln, abwickeln
shameful	beschämend, schändlich
sheepish	belämmert *fam*, verlegen, kleinlaut
shriek *v*	kreischen, schreien
shrug *v*	die Achseln zucken
sibling rivalry	Geschwisterrivalität
siblings *pl*	Geschwister
sideboard	Anrichte
sigh *v*	seufzen
silence	Stille
silk	Seide
sip *v*	nippen
skinny	dünn, mager
slumped	zusammengesackt
smooth *v*	glätten
snap *v*	blaffen, anschnauzen
sneak *v* **away**	sich davonstehlen
sneer *v*	hämisch grinsen
sniff *v*	schniefen, schnüffeln
sobbing	Schluchzen; schluchzend
society pages *pl*	Klatschseiten
solicitor	Rechtsanwalt
solve *v* **sth.**	etw. lösen
sorrow	Kummer, Leid

sparkle *v*	funkeln, glitzern
speed (sped, sped) *v* **off**	davonbrausen
spread (spread, spread) *v*	verbreiten
squat *v*	sich (hin)hocken
squeeze *v*	drücken
stacked	gestapelt
staff	Personal
stare *v*	(an)starren
startle *v* **sb.**	jmd. erschrecken
state *v*	sagen, erklären
stay *v* **over**	bei jmd. übernachten
stern	ernst
stocks *pl*	Aktien
strike (struck, struck) *v* **sb.**	jmd. schlagen
stroke *v*	streicheln
stroll *v*	schlendern
suggest *v* **sth.**	etw. vorschlagen
subconscious	Unterbewusstsein
successful	erfolgreich
suffer *v*	leiden
summon *v*	herbeizitieren, hereinrufen
support	Unterstützung, Halt
support *v*	*hier:* finanzieren; unterstützen
suppose *v*	annehmen
surround *v*	im Zusammenhang stehen mit, umgeben
survival	Überleben
survive *v*	überleben, bestehen
surviving	überlebend
suspect	Verdächtige(r)
suspect *v*	verdächtigen; misstrauisch
suspicious	verdächtig
sympathetically	mitfühlend, teilnahmsvoll
take *v* **a back seat** *fig*	in den Hintergrund treten
take *v* **advantage of**	ausnutzen, sich zunutze machen

tension	Anspannung
terms and conditions *pl*	Geschäftsbedingungen
there's more to this than meets the eye *fig*	es steckt mehr dahinter (…, als es den Anschein hat) *fig*
thoughtful(ly)	nachdenklich
threaten *v*	(be)drohen
tissue	(Papier-)Taschentuch
toss *v* **and turn** *v*	sich hin und her wälzen
trail	Spur
trapped	gefangen, eingeschlossen
tray	Tablett
treat *v* **sb. to sth.**	jmd. zu etw. einladen
turn *v* **a blind eye** *fig*	ein Auge zudrücken *fig*
unconscious	bewusstlos
underage	minderjährig
under arrest	festgenommen, verhaftet, in Haft
unlikely	unwahrscheinlich
unlisted number	Geheimnummer
untidy	unordentlich, durcheinander
upset (upset, upset) *v* **sb.**	jmd. aufregen, aus der Fassung bringen
urgent	dringend
victim	Opfer
violence	Gewalt
voluntarily	freiwillig
vouch *v* **for sb.**	für jmd. bürgen
wealthy	vermögend, wohlhabend
whisper *v*	flüstern
will	Testament
wink *v*	zwinkern
wipe *v*	abwischen
witness	Zeuge
wobble *v*	wackeln
yawn *v*	gähnen
yell *v*	brüllen, schreien